CW00665358

ITALIAN
COOK BOOK

Adopted from the Italian

of

PELLEGRINO ARTUSI

by

OLGA RAGUSA

Martino Publishing
Mansfield Centre, CT
2012

Martino Publishing
P.O. Box 373,
Mansfield Centre, CT 06250 USA

www.martinopublishing.com

ISBN   978-1-61427-287-8

© *2012 Martino Publishing*

All rights reserved. No new contribution to this publication may
be reproduced, stored in a retrieval system, or transmitted, in any form or
by any means, electronic, mechanical, photocopying, recording, or otherwise,
without the prior permission of the Publisher.

Cover design by T. Matarazzo

Printed in the United States of America On 100% Acid-Free Paper

ITALIAN
COOK BOOK

Adopted from the Italian

of

PELLEGRINO ARTUSI

by

OLGA RAGUSA

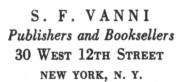

S. F. VANNI
Publishers and Booksellers
30 WEST 12TH STREET
NEW YORK, N. Y.

COPYRIGHT 1945
BY S. F. VANNI
PRINTED IN THE U. S. A.

1 — BROTH

For broth place the meat in cold water and let it boil very slowly without allowing it to overflow. (If, instead of a tasty broth, some tasty boiled meat is preferred, place meat in water already boiling). It is a known fact that spongy bones make a tasty broth, but not a nutritious one.

While the meat is boiling, place a small bunch of aromatic herbs in the pot, consisting of the lower parts of celery, carrots, parsley and basil. Some people prefer to add a piece of onion, broiled on charcoal. If one likes to color the broth in French style, one should add to it a little sugar solution prepared as follows: Place some sugar in a small pan: as soon as it gets brown, dilute it in cold water, then allow it to boil till it is completely liquified, and place it in a bottle so that it can be used whenever broth is to be colored.

A good method to preserve broth from one day to another in hot weather is to bring it to a boiling point morning and evening, and when cool, to place it in the frigidaire.

2 — BROTH FOR SICK PEOPLE

The usual amount is 4 pounds of meat for a quart of wholesome and nutritious broth. Slice thinly either lean veal or beef meat and place it in layers (one over the other) in a large pot. Sprinkle sufficient salt on it and pour enough cold water on it to cover the meat. Cover the pot with a deep dish in which some water is constantly kept. Allow the contents to simmer continuously for six hours. At the end of this time, increase the heat and cause it to boil violently for ten minutes. Strain the broth through a fine cloth.

3 — GELATIN *(or Meat Jelly)*

Boneless meat (see No. 200), about 17 ounces (500 grams)
Milkfed veal feet, about 6 ounces (150 grams)
The feet of two or three chickens
Two heads and necks of chicken

Brown the chicken feet on the fire and cut them into small pieces; then place all the ingredients into about five quarts of cold water; add enough salt and allow it to boil slowly for about seven or eight hours while skimming it often enough so that it will be free from unpalatable froth. When the liquid has boiled down to about half the original amount, pour the contents into a pan or pot, and when it has cooled off, remove the congealed fat from the surface. At this point the gelatin is already done.

However, to give the gelatin a clear shade, grind an ounce and a half of lean veal meat; place it in a pan and add an egg and two tablespoonfuls of water. Mix this well and throw the cold jelly into it. Place the pot on the fire and stir constantly and energetically till it reaches the boiling point. Then allow it to simmer for twenty minutes. While the gelatin is boiling, place a lump of sugar in a metal spoon, add a few drops of water and hold it over the fire till the sugar becomes almost black. Pour this liquid into the boiling jelly little by little till the desired shade of amber color is attained. Some people prefer to add a small glass of marsala wine.

Now take a clean towel, soak it in water and wring it out thoroughly, and while the jelly is still hot, strain it through the wet towel and fill the forms. In the Summer it is advisable to place the forms on ice so that the jelly will solidify.

To take the jelly out of the form, place a towel soaked in boiling water around the form and the jelly will detach itself and fall into the dish prepared for the purpose.

Be sure that the meat jelly is clear and transparent, and of a shade resembling topaz. It is ordinarily served with capon in gelatin or with cold cuts. It is also a nutritious dish for sick people. If consumption of the meat jelly is slow and it turns sour, this can be remedied by bringing it to a boil again.

4 — BEEF GRAVY

Cover the bottom of a pot with slices of salt pork or dry meat (the latter is to be preferred). Cut a big onion, a carrot and a sprig of celery into small pieces and make a layer of these on top of the meat, adding pieces of butter here and there. Place some slices of lean beef meat on top of this. Any kind of beef meat will serve the purpose, but for economy, the neck of the animal together with kitchen pick ups, such as cold boiled meat etc., can be used. Season the meat with salt and two pinches of clove, and place the pot on a slow fire. As soon at the onion has become brown, turn the meat. When the meat is very well browned on both sides, pour a ladleful of cold water on it. As this water dries up in the slow boiling, add another ladleful of cold water and then a third when the water in the pot has evaporated. Now it is time to add about three quarts of hot water (for about a little over a pound of meat) or, preferably bone soup, and to allow it to boil slowly for five or six hours, so that the meat juice becomes well concentrated in the broth. Strain the liquid through a fine sieve, and as soon as the fat is congealed on the surface, remove the fat. This gravy can be kept for several days, and may be consumed in various ways. It is an excellent ingredient for seasoning macaroni pudding, etc.

The flavor can be improved by adding to the meat two or more heads of chicken, cut into small pieces. The meat can be utilized in making meat balls, or other meat dishes.

5 — TOMATO GRAVY

There is a difference between tomato gravy and tomato sauce. We will talk about the tomato sauce in another section. Suffice it to say now that tomato gravy is made by simply boiling tomatoes and straining them through a fine sieve. A few small pieces of celery and a leaf or two of parsley and basil will add a fine taste to the gravy.

6 — CAPPELLETTI IN THE STYLE OF ROMAGNA

The name Cappelletti derives from their shape which resembles that of a small hat. The description that follows is the simplest way for making them, which is also the best one for digestion.

Ricotta (sweet cottage cheese) or, if preferred, one half ricotta and one half
    Italian junket, about 7 ounces (180 grams).
One half breast of capon, fried in butter, seasoned with salt and pepper, and
    cut into small pieces.
Grated Parmesan cheese, about one ounce
A whole egg, and the yolk of another egg.
Nutmeg
A little spice
Lemon rind
A pinch of salt

Taste the mixture, and if necessary, adjust the amount of the ingredients to make the stuffing as tasty as desired. If capon meat is not on hand, two ounces of leg of pork, also fried in butter and ground finely, will serve the purpose.

If the ricotta or the junket is too soft, eliminate the white of the egg from the mixture; while if it be found too hard, add another yolk to soften it.

This mixture is to be put between a wafer-like dough, which is prepared as follows:

Take enough flour and add to it enough eggs so that it can be mixed into a well beaten dough Be sure that the dough is soft, but taut enough so that it can be rolled into a thin, sheet-like wafer. Then cut it into disc-like shapes, 2½ inches in diameter.

Place a good sized pinch of the mixture in the center of the disc and fold the disc, thus forming the shape of a half moon; now join the two extreme ends of the half moon, and the cappelletto is completed. When the dough dries up, it can be moistened by placing the finger tips in water and wetting the edge of the disc.

The cappelletti ought to be boiled in a sufficient amount of capon soup and eaten together with the soup. A good eater ordinarily will eat no more than two dozen cappelletti, for they are very nutritious.

7 — TORTELLINI, ITALIAN STYLE
(Agnellotti)

Thin slices of leg of pork, about 11 ounces (300 grams)
The whole brains of a lamb, or half the brains of a larger animal
Marrow, about 2 ounces (50 grams)
Grated Parmesan cheese, about 2 ounces (50 grams)
Three yolks of egg, or one entire egg and two yolks
Nutmeg.

Fry the boneless pork with butter and a pinch of pepper. If preferred, instead of pork, less than 8 ounces of white meat from the breast of a turkey can be used equally well.

Grind this meat finely, boil the brains remove the membrane which surrounds them, and mix with the raw marrow and the other ingredients described above.

Prepare a thin dough in the same manner as for

the cappelletti (No. 6), cut it into discs, 1½ inches in diameter, and enclose the already prepared stuffing in them, folding the dough as for the cappelletti.

8 — TORTELLINI A LA BOLOGNESE
(Bologna Style)

When we hear praises sung in honor of the Bolognese kitchen, we should not think them exaggerated for they are well deserved. We may say that because of the climate of the region, its cuisine is a bit rugged, but it is certainly wholesome and tasty. The people of the city fare quite well with their manner of eating and longevity is prevalent in that region.

The Tortellini below may seem simpler and sturdier in nature than those already described, but as for wholesomeness, they are equally to be recommended.

Prosciutto (ham) not too lean, about 1 ounce (30 grams)
Mortadella of Bologna (Bologna salami), less than 1 ounce (20 grams)
Marrow, a little over 2 ounces (60 grams)
Grated Parmesan cheese, about 2 ounces (60 grams)
Egg, one
Nutmeg (no salt or pepper needed).

Grind the ham and the mortadella, brown the marrow on the fire and grind it also add the rest of the ingredients, and place everythink in the egg. Mix very well.

Prepare the same kind of dough as for the cappelletti (No. 6), cut it into even smaller discs than for the tortellini (No. 7) and put in the stuffing, folding the dough in the same manner as for the others.

The ingredients described are sufficient for the making of 300 tortellini, and three eggs mixed with flour are sufficient for the needed amount of dough. Boil the tortellini in capon soup, and serve hot.

9 — PANATA

(A sort of bread pudding served in soup)

For a serving of six portions:

Grated bread, 5 ounces
Eggs, 4
Grated Parmesan cheese, less than 2 ounces
Nutmeg
A pinch of salt

This is a dish which takes the lead on the Easter Sunday dinner table in Romagna. There they call it *tridura*. The Florentines also used to call it by that name, but this is no longer heard in the Florence of our days. However, we know that in the XIV Century *tridura* was used as a symbol of submission by the people of Cafaggiolo, near Florence. They used to place a considerable quantity of *tridura* in a brand new shining pail, place a few sticks crosswise on the edge of the pail, top it all with ten pounds of pork meat and decorate the vase with laurel leaves. Such was the gift sent to the monks of Lettino as a token of submission. Now the custom is no longer known and the name of the dish is different, but the ingredients that make the pudding are still the same.

Place the ingredients in a large pan and mix them into a rather hard compound. If too soft, add as much grated bread as necessary to give solidity.

Pour as much warm soup as is needed to moisten the mixture into the pan, place the pan on a slow fire and keep stirring, for a while. While on the fire, waiting to bring it to the boiling point, loosen the pudding from around the wall of the pan and make a heap of it in the center, without removing the pan from the fire. As soon as the panata has solidified in the pan, remove it into the soup bowl and serve it. A well made panata will form into little bunches, like grapes, in the clear soup in which it is served. Some people prefer to mix it with vegetables or peas. In that case cook these separately and mix them with the panata just before loosening it in the soup.

10 — NOODLES OF WHEAT

These are not very different from the ones made with plain flour, but they require a longer time for boiling. A good feature of these noodles is that the soup in which they are boiled will not become thick with dough substance; and they are, therefore, less heavy on the stomach.

Take the most finely ground wheat flour (semolino) and mix it with eggs, about one hour before rolling it into a fine dough. If it proves to be too soft, add a pinch or two of wheat flour so that the dough takes on the required consistency, and does not stick to the rolling pin.

11 — GNOCCHI

This is a dish to be proud of. It will serve seven or eight people.

Boil about 7 ounces of potatoes in water. Strain them through a fine sieve.

One breast of capon, boiled and ground finely
Parmesan cheese
Two yolks of eggs
Enough salt
Nutmeg

Mix all the ingredients very well. Place about 1½ ounces of flour on the board and beat the whole compound till it gets hard and taut enough to make it into long rolls, the thickness of a small finger. Cut these rolls into pieces about one inch long, and throw them into boiling soup, allowing them to boil for five or six minutes.

If the breast of capon is too big, it will be necessary to add another egg yolk in order to balance the proportions.

12 — WHOLE WHEAT PUDDING IN SOUP

A little over a glass of milk and three eggs make enough of this soup for eight people.

Boil as much whole wheat farina as desired in milk till it becomes thick. Remove it from the fire and season it with salt, grated Parmesan cheese, a piece of butter; flavor it with nutmeg and let it cool off. When cold, soften the pudding with eggs and reduce it to a creamlike liquid. Use a double boiler. Moisten the bottom of the small boiler with butter and stick a sheet of wax paper to it. Pour in the liquid, cover it well; place it in the larger boiler containing water, and place the double boiler on the fire. Wait till the compound has thickened into a solid pudding, and remove it from the fire.

When cold, take it out of the pot without breaking it. If it sticks to the pot, loosen it with a thin blade. Cut it into either square or oblong pieces of one inch and two inches in diameter respectively. Let these boil in soup for a couple of minutes and serve.

13 — SOUP OF PARADISE

This is a substantial and delicious dish, but as for its heavenly quality, that seems a little far-fetched to me.

Beat up four whites of eggs and add the yolks to them, four tablespoonfuls of hard finely-grated bread and four spoonfuls of grated Parmesan cheese. Flavor all with nutmeg.

Mix slowly so that the compound will remain soft and pour it, one spoonful at a time, into boiling soup. Let it boil for seven or eight minutes, and serve.

The above quantity is sufficient for six people.

14 — SOUP WITH SHREDDED MEAT

Lean milkfed veal, about 6 ounces
Fat ham, about 1 ounce
Grated Parmesan cheese, less than 2 ounces
Plain bread pudding, made with bread crumbs, water, a piece of butter, 2 spoonfuls
Eggs, 1
Nutmeg
Sufficient salt and ham

Grind the meat very finely and strain it through a fine sieve. Mix it with the egg and the other ingred-

— 19 —

ients, and as soon as the soup boils, pour the mixture in by spoonfuls. When boiled, serve the soup.

The above quantity is sufficient for four or five servings, but it can be made to suffice for 12 people by extending it as follows: Cut some stale bread into small squares, the size of dice; place these into a pan with some fat, and brown them quickly on the fire. When you are about to serve the soup, place these browned squares into a soup bowl and pour the above soup with shredded meat on top of them.

15 — SOUP WITH RICOTTA
(*Sweet cottage cheese*)

Make the same compound as described in No. 6 for the cappelletti, but instead of enclosing it in foliated dough, throw it into the boiling soup, spoonful by spoonful. As soon as it becomes hard, serve it.

16 — SOUP WITH SEMOLINO
(*Wholewheat*) NUTS

Milk, less than 1 pint
Semolino (wholewheat), less than 3 ounces
Grated Parmesan cheese, about 1 ounce
Eggs, 1 whole egg and the yolk of another
Butter, 1 square inch
Salt
Nutmeg

Place the milk and piece of butter on the fire. As soon as it boils, add the semolino pinch by pinch. Salt it. When it is sufficiently cooked and still hot, but not boiling, add the egg and the yolk, the Parmesan cheese, and the nutmeg flavor. Allow it to become cold. Spread it into an elongated strip ¾ of an inch wide. Cut it into small pieces, the size of a peanut and roll these into balls. Boil these balls in soup for a short time and serve them.

The amount of flour ordinarily absorbed by the compound is about one ounce, varying with the softness or hardness of the mixture. This quantity is usually sufficient for six people.

17 — SOUP WITH RICOTTA TILES

(*Mattoncini*)

Ricotta (Italian sweet cottage cheese), about 7 ounces
Grated Parmesan cheese, less than 1 ounce
Eggs, 2
Salt, flavor of lemon rinds, and nutmeg.

Mash the ricotta well and strain it through a fine sieve. Add the other ingredients, adding the eggs one at a time while mixing. Beat everything very well. Using a double boiler place a sheet of wax paper on the bottom of the small boiler and pour the mixture on it. Cover it well, place it in the larger boiler and set it on the fire. When it has cooked sufficiently, allow it to get cold and take it out of the pot unbroken. Cut it into small squares of about ¼ inch. Place these in the soup bowl, pour the soup on them and serve.

This quantity is ordinarily enough for six people.

18 — SOUP OF ANGEL BREAD

Crustless white bread, less than 6 ounces
Ham, not too lean, less than 2 ounces
Marrow, about 1½ ounces
Enough flour
Eggs, 1 whole egg and the yolk of another
Nutmeg
Grated Parmesan, 1½ ounces

Soak the crustless bread slightly in boiling soup; squeeze it thoroughly in a towel. Grind the ham; flatten the marrow with a knife blade and chop it till it looks like thick jelly. Mix these three ingredients with the Parmesan, and add the eggs.

Sprinkle some flour on the pastry board thinly and place the compound on it. Spread more flour on top and beat the compound while adding more flour, till it has absorbed about 3 ounces. Make balls as large as peanuts. Boil them in soup for ten minutes and serve.

This amount is ordinarily enough for ten or twelve people.

19 — SOUP OF POTATO BALLS

Potatoes, a little more than a pound
Butter, about 1½ ounces
Grated Parmesan cheese, 1½ ounces
Egg Yolks, 3
Nutmeg

Boil the potatoes and peel them. Strain them through a fine sieve and salt them. Add the rest of the ingredients and mix well. Sprinkle flour on the pastry board and place the compound on it. Make thin long rolls with the mixture and cut these into pieces the size of a peanut. Shape them into little balls. Fry these in oil or lard as for French fried potatoes. Place the fried balls in the soup bowl, pour boiling soup on them and serve.

This quantity is ordinarily sufficient for eight persons.

20 — SOUP WITH RICE BALLS

Rice, a little more than 3 ounces
Butter, less than 1 ounce
Grated Parmesan cheese, less than 1 ounce
One yolk of egg
Nutmeg
Salt

Boil the rice in milk till it has thickened. Before removing it from the fire, add butter and salt. Remove it from the fire and as soon as it has stopped boiling, add the remainder of the ingredients. As for the rest of the process, follow the instructions as given for recipe No. 19. These rice balls are even tastier than the potato balls.

This quantity is ordinarily enough for eight persons.

21 — A TWO-COLOR SOUP

Flour, about 6 ounces
Butter, more than 2 ounces
Grated Parmesan cheese, less than 1 ounce
Milk, less than a pint
Eggs, two whole eggs and two yolks
Salt to taste
Nutmeg
A handful of spinach

This is a most delicate soup, a favorite with the ladies of Tuscany; but it would be out of place in Romagna where people, preferring more substantial dishes, would even scoff at tapioca.

Boil the spinach, squeeze the water from it and strain it through a fine sieve. Place the butter in a pot, melt it on the fire and mix the flour with it. Beat well. Warm the milk and add it slowly. Salt it, and while boiling, mix it well into an evenly worked compound. Remove it from the fire. Wait till it becomes tepid and add the eggs. Mix well and add the Parmesan and the flavor of nutmeg.

Divide the compound into two equal parts. Take one part and add enough strained spinach to it. Mix well till the green of the spinach has evenly permeated the whole compound. Now place the yellow compound into a pastry gun or tube (cake decorator) having round openings, and squeeze it into boiling soup (as with passatelli No. 32). Repeat the operation with the spinach compound and serve the soup.

This quantity is sufficient for eight or ten people.

22 — STUFFED SOUP

Half a breast of a capon or of a large chicken
A small slice of ham (not too lean)
A small piece of marrow

Chop these three ingredients together; season the compound with grated Parmesan and flavor it with nutmeg. Add an egg and mix everything well. No salt is needed.

Cut some stale bread into oblong slices of about

½x3 inches. Remove the crust from one half of the slices and spread the compound on them. Now, to each of these add the slice with the crust; press the two together till they adhere well. Cut the slices into small squares and fry them in pure lard, oil or butter, according to the prevailing taste and usage. Before serving, place the squares into a soup bowl and pour boiling soup on them.

23 — SPLIT PEA SOUP

Since the peas must be strained through a sieve, one need not be too particular about their tenderness. Less than one pound will be enough for six servings, especially if the diners eat soup for style's sake, and not as a main dish.

Boil the peas in soup. Make the usual little aromatic bunch of celery, parsley, carrot and a sprig of basil; immerse it in the boiling soup for a short time and remove it. When the peas have boiled sufficiently, fry two slices of stale bread in butter and add to the soup. Strain everything through a fine sieve. Dilute the mixture with ordinary soup; add a little meat gravy of some kind. Cut stale bread into small squares; fry them in butter. The diced bread is to be thrown into the pea soup while eating it.

24 — SOUP A LA SANTE'

This soup is made with a variety of vegetables. Carrots, sorrel, celery and white cabbage are the usual ingredients. Cut the white cabbage into the shape of noodles, place it on the fire and remove it as soon as it has oozed water; then squeeze out the water thoroughly. Cut the carrots and celery into pieces of about ¾ of an inch. Clean sorrel grass and place everything on the fire to steam. Add a pinch of salt, pepper and a piece of butter. As soon as the vegetables have absorbed the butter, add enough water and allow them to boil. Using stale white bread, cut it into dice-like pieces and fry them in either virgin oil, butter or pure lard. For economy place a large quantity of fat in the pan and throw the bread squares into it when it is boiling at good speed. Another way of preparing the bread is to cut it into slices of about two inches; toast it dry and cut into small squares. Place the diced bread in the soup bowl, pour the boiling soup with vegetables on it and serve at once.

25 — SOUP WITH MEAT GRAVY

The success of this soup depends on the making of a palatable meat gravy.

Taking as point of departure a quantity sufficient for four people, a little more than one pound of beef (suitable for gravy), and one or two chicken necks, together with some meat pick-ups from the kitchen, is enough to make a tasty gravy. Besides the gravy, one must have plenty of vegetables. These vary with the season, but ordinarily celery, carrots, black cabbage, sorrel, summer squash, peas, and one potato make the desired combination.

Cut the squash into small pieces but cut the rest of the vegetables into noodle-like strips. Boil them till tender; fry them in butter and soak them in meat gravy. Cut some bread into slices about two inches long: toast it, and cut it in small squares.

Arrange the bread squares and the other ingredients in a soup bowl as follows: A layer of diced toasted bread; then a layer of vegetables and a dash of grated Parmesan cheese. Repeat the operation till you have used up the entire amount. Finally pour sufficient gravy on it and without jarring, cover the dish and place it in a hot oven for about half an hour. Then serve it. Since the ingredients will absorb the gravy, it is necessary to keep some gravy in order to add it to the dish just before serving it at the dinner table.

26 — SOUP WITH EGG BREAD

This is not an elaborate soup, but it is popular with foreign people.

Eggs, 3
Flour, a little over 1 ounce
A square or two of butter

First beat the egg yolks together with the flour and butter. Beat the egg whites separately and add them to the mixture. Cover the bottom of a cake pan with a sheet of wax paper; pour the dough on it and bake it in the oven. When this bread is baked and it has cooled off, cut it into small squares, and place these in a soup bowl; pour the boiling soup on them and serve with Parmesan cheese.

This quantity is sufficient for six or seven diners.

27 — QUEEN SOUP

The name of this soup suggests the idea that it ought to be the best soup of all, but we can only say that it is one of the most delicious dishes. It is ordinarily made with the white meat of a broiled chicken.

Remove the shells from six almonds and grind the almonds finely together with the white meat of the chicken. Soak one crustless slice of bread for each half pound of meat in milk or in hot soup and add it to the mixture. Mix well and strain the compound through a fine sieve. Place it in a soup bowl and dilute it all with a ladleful of hot soup. Cut the usual bread squares in dice-like shape. fry them in butter and throw them into the soup bowl. Pour in the boiling soup, mix well and serve with Parmesan cheese.

The opportune time to make this soup is when, after a big meal, one has plenty of broiled chicken left over. The almonds are added to give the soup a milky color, but do not allow the soup to thicken. Some people mash the yolk of a boiled egg and add it to the soup.

28 — RICE, HUNTER STYLE

This tasty and substantial dish can be prepared as follows:

Cut an entire chicken into pieces, except the head and feet. Fry a clove of garlic in salt pork and parsley, and as it takes on color, add the chicken, a piece of butter, a pinch of salt and a little pepper. As soon as the chicken has become brown, throw it into boiling water, and add the rice immediately after. When the rice is about to be removed from the fire, add a dash of Parmesan cheese..

Instead of the salt pork, some sort of chopped smoked pork meat may serve the purpose. A little tomato sauce or tomato paste can also be used, but whatever one does in the way of seasoning. one should not allow the rice to overcook. Neither should the rice be served before it has thoroughly absorbed the water.

29 — RICE AND SAUSAGE

Boil the rice in a broth into which slices of sausage have been cut. Do not wash the rice, but simply clean and put it in a cloth to remove the dust. Turnips or cabbage can be added to the rice and sausage. These must be half cooked before they are added. Cut the turnips into small squares, the cabbage into slices, and fry them in butter. Shortly before taking the rice off the fire, add a goodly pinch of Parmesan cheese to tie it together better and to season it.

30 — CUSCUS

The following quantity should be enough for six or seven persons.

A slice of breast of veal, 1 lb. 10 oz. (750 grams)
Lean boneless veal, 5 oz., (150 grams)
Coarse-grained semolino, 10 oz., (300 grams)
One chicken liver
One hard boiled egg
The yolk of an egg
Various greens, such as onions, cabbage, celery, carrots, spinach, beets, etc.

Place the semolino in a wide and shallow earthenware pot or in a copper baking - pan; season it with a pinch of salt and pepper, and while pouring two inches of water on it, drop by drop, grind it with the palm of the hand to dilute it. After the water pour on a spoonful of oil bit by bit, and continue to grind it in the same manner, taking more than half an hour for the first and second operations. When the semolino has been seasoned in this way, put it into a soup plate and cover it with a cloth, the ends of which should be tied under the plate.

Put the slice of veal on the fire with 3 quarts of water to make a broth, and when it has been skimmed, cover it with the soup plate already prepared, in such a way that the broth does not touch the plate. The openings of the two pots must coincide so that no smoke can escape. Leave the semolino in this way for an hour and a quarter, steaming it. Remove the cloth from the dish when half-cooked to mix it, and then put it back as before.

Chop the 5 oz. of lean meat with a knife, add a piece of crustless bread cut into small pieces, season with salt and pepper, make meat balls not much bigger than acorns from it, and fry them in oil.

Chop the greens a little and first fry the onion in oil until it has turned brown. Add the other vegetables, season them with salt and pepper, mix them often, and let them absorb the water they ooze out. When they are nearly dry, wet them with meat sauce or broth and tomato sauce, and let them cook together with the chicken liver cut into small pieces and the meat balls.

Put the semolino on the fire in a casserole and without letting it boil, dissolve the egg yolk in it and pour part of the vegetable mixture into it. Mix it and when it is dry pour it on a platter so that it falls into a form; decorate this with slices of the hard-boiled egg. Add the rest of the vegetable mixture to the broth in the pot and send it to the table divided into as many cups as there are diners. Every diner puts a portion of semolino on his plate and eats it with the broth.

The slice of veal is served later as boiled meat.

31 — MINESTRONE

This is not a dish for a weak or too delicate stomach, though it is palatable and nourishing when properly prepared. The following quantity is ordinarily sufficient for four or five people.

Boil the soup meat as usual. Cook a handful of beans (possibly fresh beans) separately in same soup. If the beans are not fresh, it is advisable to boil them in plain water before placing them in the soup. Cut some black cabbage into thin narrow strips. Cut a little spinach and some beets into small pieces and soak these vegetables in fresh water for a while. Stew the vegetables (without adding water) in a pot till they have oozed out all the water, and drain this water from them. Chop about 1½ ounces of ham (not too lean) together with a clove of garlic, a sprig of parsley, and fry this separately on a low fire. Cut a potato into small pieces, also some celery, a carrot, one squash, and a small onion and add everything to the vegetable pot. Add also the beans, and a little tomato gravy or tomato paste if desired. Season all with a pinch of salt and pepper and place it in the boiling meat soup. Finally, add enough rice so that the minestrone is not too thin. Before removing it from the fire, throw in a goodly dash of Parmesan cheese.

32 — PASSATELLI MADE WITH FARINA

The following quantity is enough for six persons.

Farina (or fine whole wheat flour), about 5 ounces
Grated Parmesan cheese, 1 ounce
Milk, a little over a pint
Eggs, two whole eggs and two egg yolks
Salt, nutmeg, and lemon rinds

Boil the farina in milk, and if it is too thin add enough to thicken it. Salt it as soon as it has sufficiently boiled. Allow it to cool and add the eggs and the rest of the ingredients.

Place the compound in a cake decorator having somewhat large round holes at the end, and squeeze it into the boiling soup. Allow it to boil till the *passatelli* have hardened, and serve.

33 — RICE WITH FRESH SQUASH

Take as much fresh squash as rice and cut it into small pieces of about ¾ of an inch. Fry the squash in butter, add enough salt and a little pepper. As soon as the squash is browned, add it to the half-cooked rice, and allow the two to cook together.

The rice should remain somewhat thin and the squash must not be overdone. If instead of soup, plain water is used, allow the rice to absorb the water and then flavor it w th tomato sauce (No. 78) by adding the tomato uce when the squash is thrown into the rice.

34 --- TORTELLI

This is a recipe for three adults.

Ricotta, Italian junket, or both mixed, about 7 ounces
Grated Parmesan cheese, about 1½ cunces
Flavor of nutmeg, some spices, and a pinch of salt
A little chopped parsley
Eggs, 1 whole egg and the yolk of another

Mix all the ingredients well and enclose the mixture in a pastry dough prepared and cut in the same way as that for the Cappelletti (No. 6). Put sufficient water on the fire; when it is boiling, add enough salt, and throw in the tortellini. When these have cooked, drain the water off well, place them into a dish and while hot, add some butter and grated cheese, and serve.

35 — MASHED PEA SOUP WITH LEAN MEAT

The following is a recipe for six people.

Mashed fresh green peas, about 14 ounces
Ham, about 1½ ounces
Butter, about 1½ ounces
One small new onion
One small carrot

Chop the ham finely; add the other ingredients to it, and chop them all together till the mixture is very well mashed. Place it on a slow fire and add butter, a bit of salt and very little pepper. When browned, pour in sufficient water. As soon as it reaches the boiling point, add the peas and allow it to cook. Strain through a sieve. Prepare the toasted bread as for recipe No. 23 and throw the bread in at the time of serving the minestra.

In Winter, dry peas can be used instead. provided they are prepared and mashed as if fresh. It is also well to toast a couple of slices of bread, boil them together with the peas, and pass it all through the sieve. This will give body to the soup.

36 — BEAN SOUP

It is often said that beans are the poor man's meat. Beans satisfy and keep hunger away for a longer period of time than meat. Even this lowly dish can be prepared palatably if one follows these simple directions:

Choose beans with thin shells, or if this is not possible, strain the beans through a sieve when cooked. For five people prepare a sort of fricassee with the following ingredients: ¼ of an onion, a clove of garlic, a few sprigs of parsley, and a goodly piece of white celery. Chop these very finely and place them on a slow fire with a good measure of olive oil and a dash of pepper. As soon as the fry has taken on a brownish color, add two ladlefuls of soup from the bean pot. Add some tomato sauce or tomato paste, and as it comes to the boiling point, throw this mixture into the bean pot. While waiting for the bean soup to absorb the flavor, toast the bread as usual and cut it into dice-like pieces, to be put into the soup individually at table. Those preferring vegetables, can add boiled black cabbage to the fricassee.

37 — LENTILS SOUP

If the legend has it that Esau sold his birthright for a plate of lentils, it must be granted that this food was a favorite even in ancient times. Evidently Esau was partial to lentils, since he considered them more valuable that the privileges of his birthright. At any rate, the taste of lentils has a certain delicacy which makes them more palatable than beans to some people. As for digestibility, they are quite desirable.

Lentils soup is prepared like bean soup (No. 36). Prepare the same sort of fricassee, toast and dice the bread. If it is desired to add rice to the soup, use more water. The surplus water will be absorbed by the rice, and the soup will have more body. Ordinarily, the rice is cooked separately in lentil water. The thickness of the soup can be regulated at pleasure when adding the rice.

38 — FROG SOUP

Two dozen large frogs make enough soup for five or six servings.

Cut off the frogs' legs and lay them aside. Grind and mash together well two cloves of garlic, some parsley, a carrot, celery and basil. Instead of garlic, onions can be used. Place the mixture on a slow fire with a goodly measure of olive oil and a dash of pepper. When the garlic has turned brown, add the frogs. Turn the frogs often enough to prevent them from sticking to the pot. When the frogs have absorbed a good deal of the oil, add a few pieces of fresh tomatoes or some diluted tomato paste. Allow this to boil for a while and then add enough water to cover the contents. Boil till the frogs are well done, in fact, overdone. Strain the soup through a sieve so that only the bones of the frogs are left. Now place a portion of this strained soup in a small pot together with the frogs' legs, set aside in the beginning, and allow it to boil a while. Remove the bones from the legs; soak a few dry mushrooms well, and add them to the soup together with the legs. Toast and dice the bread; serve it with the soup.

39 — SOUP WITH BROTH OF MULLET

Mullet is one of the fish best suited for a good broth. If this cannot be obtained, Grayling can be used; the meat of this fish, though it will not produce the tasty broth of mullet, will be of a fine quality and more digestible.

For seven or eight persons take a mullet weighing at least 2 lbs., scrape off the scales, clean it, and boil it.

Mix a generous quantity of parsley, garlic, onion, carrots, celery, and put this on the fire with oil, salt and pepper. When it has taken on color cover it with tomato sauce and let it boil together with the broth of the fish. Strain the broth and with some of it cook a small quantity of celery, carrots, and dried mushrooms—all cut into small pieces. This will serve to give aroma.

Toast the bread for the soup and cut it into squares, put it into the soup-tureen and pour the boiling broth with the above-named flavoring over it, Serve with Parmesan cheese.

40 — GRAYLING SOUP AND PASTINE OR NOODLES

Grayling by its very nature is a delicate sort of fish. Boil it in plain water in order to preserve its flavor. It makes a most delicious soup. The following ingredients will make enough soup for three or four persons.

Grayling, a little more than 1 lb.
Pastine, or fine noodless, about 4 ounces
Butter, one ounce or more
Water, a little more than 1 qt.

Place the grayling on the fire in the quart of cold water and salt it. As soon as the fish is cooked, pass the contents through a strainer and set the strained soup on the fire again. As it boils, add the rest of the ingredients, except the butter, and flavor it with a little tomato in order to destroy the fishy taste. Place the butter in the soupbowl and pour in the soup. Serve with Parmesan cheese.

41 — SOUP OF MASHED DRY PEAS

A recipe for ten or twelve persons.
If the quantity of peas is a little over one pint

(½ quart), place them in about two and a half quarts of water and set them to boil on a slow fire. While the peas are boiling make a fricassee by chopping together ½ of an onion, one carrot, two pieces of celery each about 2 inches in length, and possibly a little anise.

Place a piece of butter in a pot; add the fricassee and allow it to brown on a low fire. As soon as it is browned, drain the water from the half cooked peas and pour them into the fricassee. Add a pinch of salt and pepper and allow them to boil till the fricassee has been absorbed by the peas. Add more pea water and allow it to boil till the peas are well done. Strain the contents through a sieve, and if it is too thick, dilute it with warm water. Taste it, and if necessary, add a piece of butter. Cut bread into little squares, fry them in butter, and serve them with the soup.

42 — TAGLIATELLE WITH HAM GRAVY
(Large noodles)

Since the tagliatelle must be boiled in water and drained dry in order to be seasoned with ham gravy, they must be made with a thicker pastry dough and cut into a larger size than the usual soup noodles. The dough is made, as usual, with flour and eggs. No water is required.

Cut a generous slice of ham into small squares; chop a quantity of celery and carrot equal to that of the ham. Place the above ingredients in a pot together with enough butter and set it on a low fire. As soon as the contents take on a brownish color, add some tomato or tomato paste together with a ladleful of soup; if there is no soup available, water will do as well.

Boil the tagliatelle with very little salt. Be sure they are not overdone. Drain the water from them thoroughly and season them with the ham gravy and Parmesan cheese. When sausages are in season, they may be used in place of ham. Some people prefer adding a piece of butter to the gravy when removing it from the fire.

43 — GREEN TAGLIATELLE

A recipe for four or five persons.

The tagliatelle are usually prepared as a dry dish. However, green tagliatelle are more digestible than those made with flour and eggs only. Boil some spinach, squeeze the water from it, and chop it finely. Place a handful of chopped spinach and two eggs in enough flour on the pastry board. Mix well and work the dough by hand till it has become taut. Then roll the dough into a thin pastry layer with a rolling pin. While rolling it, dash some flour on the dough to prevent it from sticking. When rolled into the desired thinness, fold the dough up in a towel and wait till the moisture has dried up. Cut the dough into larger noodles than the usual soup noodles.. The sign of a well-worked dough is the length and tautness of the tagliatelle.

Cook the tagliatelle till the force of the boiling water lifts and swells them to the surface. Drain the water. Place the tagliatelle in a large dish and season them with gravy, as in No. 42 and 52, or simply with butter and cheese.

44 — TAGLIATELLE IN ROMAGNA STYLE

"Short additions and long tagliatelle" is the adage which the Bolognese are wont to repeat. This is indeed a wise saying, for while additions startle poor husbands, long tagliatelle show the cooking virtuosity of the housewife. The foreign habit of breaking the tagliatelle into bits when cooking them in soup is against our national tradition. According to our national usage, noodles and tagliatelle must be long.

For these tagliatelle in Romagna style, prepare the dough as in No. 42. Do not allow them to boil very long; drain the water thoroughly; place them in a pan and season them with the gravy described in No. 64, adding a piece of butter as large as necessary for the quantity of minestra. Place the pan on a low fire for a short time, mix well and slowly; then serve. This is a tasty minestra, but its native air is that of Romagna.

45 — BLACK RISOTTO WITH CUTTLE-FISH IN FLORENTINE STYLE

Remove the skin and the parts which cannot be used—the bones, the muscles of the mouth, the eyes, and the digestive tube. Put the bladder which contains the ink aside, wash the fish well, cut it into squares and cut the tail into small pieces.

Chop two medium-sized onions very finely, or

better still, one onion and two cloves of garlic, and put them on the fire in a casserole with plenty of fine oil. When the fricassee has taken on color, throw in the cuttle-fish and wait until it boils and begins to turn yellow. Then add about 1⅛ lbs. of beet greens, cleaned of the bigger ribs and somewhat chopped. Mix and allow to boil for about half an hour; then pour in 1⅛ lbs. of rice (about as much as there is of the fish) and the ink. When the rice has become well colored with the sauce, finish cooking it in hot water. Rice, as a general rule, must never be over-done, and when it is dry, it must remain in form on the platter on which it is served. Serve with grated cheese, but in case of delicate digestion abstain from the use of cheese with these and similar heavy ingredients.

The same kind of risotto can be made with some variations. Do not use beet greens or ink, and when the fish begins to turn yellow, pour in the rice and cook it in hot water or tomato sauce adding a bit of butter for flavoring. When it is almost done add Parmesan cheese.

Still better, when the rice and fish is two-thirds cooked add peas.

46 — RICE WITH PEAS

Rice, a little over 1 pound
Butter, 4 ounces
Enough Parmesan cheese
A medium-sized onion

To clean the rice, wash it and rub it well in a towel. Chop the onion finely and place it on a low fire with half of the butter. As soon as the onion

becomes brown, add the rice and stir it constantly till
it has completely absorbed the butter. Add hot water
by pouring in one ladleful at the time. Do not allow
the rice to cook in too little water, because it would
harden in the center of the pot, and the surface would
turn into starch dust. Add some salt and allow the
rice to boil till it has absorbed the water. When about
to remove the rice from the fire, add the remainder
of the butter and a proportionate amount of peas,
prepared as described in No. 267. Add a goodly dash
of grated Parmesan cheese and serve. This quantity.
is ordinarily sufficient for five servings.

47 — RICE WITH TOMATO SAUCE

Rice, about 18 ounces
Butter, about 4 ounces
Parmesan cheese, as much as required

Place the butter in a pot and as soon as it is melted add the rice. When the rice has absorbed the butter,.
add enough hot water spoonful by spoonful. When
the rice is half cooked, season it with the tomato sauce
described in No. 78 and allow it to cook. On removing
it from the fire, add the Parmesan cheese and serve.

48 — RISOTTO IN MILANESE STYLE I.

Rice, 18 ounces
Butter, 3½ ounces
Saffron, enough for coloring
Half of a medium-sized onion

For the cooking of the rice, follow recipe No.
46. To make this dish tasty and nutritious, it is neces-

sary to use soup. It is advisable to dilute the saffron in a little hot soup before adding it to the rice, which is usually served with Parmesan cheese at the side. Saffron stimulates appetite and helps the digestive process as well.

49 — RISOTTO IN MILANESE STYLE II.

This risotto is more elaborate and heavier on the stomach than that described in recipe No. 48. but it is much tastier.

The following ingredients are sufficient for five persons.

Rice, about 18 ounces
Butter, 3½ ounces
Marrow, less than 2 ounces
Half an onion
White wine of good quality, two thirds of a glass
Saffron, sufficient for coloring
Parmesan cheese, as much as is necessary

Chop the onion and place it on a low fire together with the marrow and half of the butter. As it becomes brown, add the rice. After a minute add the wine and let the rice cook in the soup. Before removing it from the fire, add the other half of the butter and the Parmesan. Serve it with more Parmesan at the side.

50 — RISOTTO IN MILANESE STYLE III.

Rice, 10 ounces
Butter, less than 2 ounces
¼ of a medium-sized onion
Marsala wine, ¼ of an ordinary wineglass
Saffron, enough for coloring

Chop the onion and brown it in half of the butter. Add the rice and after one minute the Marsala wine. Allow the rice to cook in the soup and when almost done, add the rest of the butter and the saffron diluted in a little soup. Add a goodly dash of Parmesan and serve.

This amount should, ordinarily, suffice for three servings.

51 — RISOTTO WITH FISH SOUP

After boiling a whole fish or a large mullet in the manner described in recipe No. 289, the strained soup can be used to prepare either risotto or other kinds of soup. Chop together $\frac{1}{4}$ of an onion, one or two cloves of garlic, parsley, some carrot and celery, and place the ingredients on the fire in sufficient oil. Add a pinch of salt and pepper. As the mixture takes on color, add some tomato sauce or tomato paste diluted in a ladleful of soup. Allow it to boil for a while and add the rice, which should be allowed to cook in the same boiling soup by adding it ladleful by ladleful to the pot. When the rice is half cooked, add a piece of butter, and when it is well done, add a dash of Parmesan. If preferred, some dry mushrooms may be added to the soup. Serve with Parmesan at side.

52 — MACARONI IN BOLOGNESE STYLE

The best macaroni are those made with semolino and left in their natural state, that is to say, without artificial coloring. For this particular kind of minestra, a rather short and thick quality, something like so-called elbow macaroni, is ordinarily used.

The following ingredients will be sufficient to make a gravy for seasoning 18 ounces of macaroni.

Lean veal meat, about 6 ounces
Smoked pork meat, 2 ounces
Butter, 1½ ounces
Onion, ¼ of a medium sized one
Celery, 2 long pieces of white celery or flavor of green celery
A pinch of flour
A small potful of soup
Very little salt, some pepper and nutmeg

Cut the meat into squares; chop the smoked pork meat, the onion and the rest of the vegetables, and set everything on a low fire together with the butter. As the meat takes on a brownish color, add flour and the soup. Allow it to boil slowly till it is well done. To improve the gravy add some dry mushrooms and a little tender liver at the beginning. If a delicate flavor is desired, add a half glass of cream when the gravy is already done.

Boil the macaroni in a large pot and in plenty of water. Be sure not to overcook them. Overcooked macaroni paste together when the water is drained. Besides, overdone macaroni are hard to digest and not so tasty. Place the macaroni in a large dish, season with plenty of gravy and a goodly dash of Parmesan cheese, and serve.

53 — MACARONI WITH SARDINES IN SICILIAN STYLE (*Fresh sardines*)

Clean the sardines, remove the heads, tails, backbones ,and split them lengthwise. Cover them thinly with flour, fry them, add a pinch of salt and set them aside. Boil the fennel, squeeze the water from it, chop it finely, and set is aside too.

A recipe for six persons.

Regular spaghetti, 18 ounces
Fresh sardines, 18 ounces
Salted Anchovies, 6
Wild fennel, about 11 ounces
Enough olive oil

Boil the spaghetti whole (without breaking them), drain the water from them and set them aside. Wash the salt from the anchovies and fry them in olive oil till they are dissolved. Add the fennel, a pinch of salt and pepper, and allow it to boil for ten minutes. In the meantime, add tomato sauce or diluted tomato paste. Now that all the ingredients are done, take a baking dish or a pie dish and season the macaroni as follows:

Alternate layers of spaghetti, and of sardine, fennel, etc. Repeat the process till you have seasoned the entire amount. Place the dish in the oven and allow it to bake. Serve while hot.

54 — MACARONI IN FRENCH STYLE

Macaroni, a little over ½ lb.
Butter, 2 oz.
Gruyere cheese, a little over 1 ounce
Parmesan cheese, 1 ounce
A pot of broth

Take long macaroni of Neapolitan style, which are better suited to this use, and cook them in slightly salted water until half done. Drain well and finish cooking them in broth. Before adding the seasoning be sure to drain the broth off well so as to put it on again later, otherwise the gruyere cheese becomes pasty and does not remain attached to the macaroni. Serve the macaroni after having kept them on the fire a bit longer to let them become juicy.

Milk can be substituted for broth.

Serve the macaroni with grated cheese for those who like their food to be spicy.

55 — MACARONI IN NEAPOLITAN STYLE

Take a piece of boneless beef, about 4x6 inches. Chop a piece of salt pork together with a clove of garlic, parsley, salt and pepper. Cut a piece of ham into thin slices, add some raisins and Indian nuts. Stuff the meat with these ingredients. Tie the meat with a strong thread to prevent loosening of the spices. Chop another piece of salt pork together with some onion; place it in a pot together with the meat and allow it to brown evenly. As soon as the salt pork has dissolved, add three of four slices of peeled tomato, and when this is done, gradually add a sufficient amount of tomato sauce. Allow it to boil slowly till it thickens. Add enough water to cover the meat, also a pinch of salt and pepper, and allow it to boil on a low fire for an hour and a half.

When fresh tomatoes are not available, canned tomato sauce or tomato paste serves the purpose as well. As for the macaroni, be sure to boil them in a large pot and in plenty of water. Do not allow them to be overdone. With this gravy and some piquant cheese the Neapolitans season their macaroni, while the meat is used as a side dish.

56 — POTATO GNOCCHI

There is quite a large family of gnocchi. I have already described soup gnocchi, but now we shall learn how to prepare other kinds of gnocchi.

Wheat flour, 6 ounces
Large potatoes, about 14 ounces

Boil or steam the potatoes and while still hot, peel them. Mash them and pass them through a fine sieve. Mix the mashed potatoes with flour and knead them well. Roll the dough into strips and cut them into pieces ½ inch long. Spray some flour on these cylindrical pieces and hollow them one by one on the back of the cheese grater with your thumb. Boil them in salted water for about ten minutes; drain the water; place them in a dish and season with cheese, butter, and tomato sauce, if desired. If a more delicate taste is desired, cook the gnocchi in milk, adding only a pinch of salt and a little Parmesan cheese.

57 — CORNFLOUR GNOCCHI

Whenever one feels a sense of discomfort due to a very substantial meal, one may neutralize the feeling at the next meal by making this minestra the main course. It is a most digestible food, especially if fol·lowed by a course of white fish.

Be sure to use a coarse kind of cornflour. The corn semolino sold in stores serves the purpose.

Set a pot of water on the fire, salt it, and as soon as the water comes to a boiling point, start to pour in the cornflour with your left hand, while stirring energetically and constantly with a long and heavy spoon in the right hand, so that no lumps are formed. As soon as the flour has thickened, remove it from the fire. Take spoonfuls of this meal-like mixture, cut it into small pieces with a knife and place it in layers in a dish, seasoning it, layer by layer, with cheese, butter and tomato sauce. Serve while hot.

58 — NOODLES WITH RABBIT SAUCE
(Pappardelle)

Wash the rabbit, cut it into pieces and put it into a saucepan to make the water ooze out. Drain and add a small piece of butter, a bit of oil and a mixture of the liver of the animal, a piece of dry meat, onion, celery, carrots, and parsley—all well chopped. Add salt and pepper. Stir often and when it is browned add water and tomato sauce to finish the cooking, putting in another piece of butter at the very end.

Use the sauce and Parmesan cheese to flavor a noodle soup and serve the rabbit as a second dish.

If the soup is not to be flavored, it is not necessary to use the dry meat in the sauce.

59 — NOODLES WITH HARE

Since the meat of the hare is dry and tasteless, it must be helped out by a meat sauce of much substance, so that a good soup can be obtained.

Here are the ingredients for soup for five persons. A dough of three eggs, cut into noodles the width of a finger should suffice; or if the noodles are bought ready-made, a little over 1 pound is enough..

The two fillets of a hare, about 7 ounces
Butter, less than 2 ounces
Dry meat, a little over 1 ounce
Half of a medium-sized onion
Half a carrot
A piece of celery
Nutmeg
Parmesan cheese
Flour, 1 tbs.
Meat juice, 1½ pts.

Remove the skin from the fillets and cut them into small pieces. Make a fricasee of the dry meat, onion, celery, and carrots. Chop well and put it on the fire with a third of the butter and the meat of the hare; season with salt and pepper. When the meat is browned, sprinkle the flour on it, and shortly after add the sauce and finish cooking it, adding the rest of the butter and the nutmeg.

Cook the noodles in salted water, drain them well, and flavor them on a plate with the Parmesan and the sauce.

If there are no fillets, use the legs.

60 — RAVIOLI

A recipe for two dozen ravioli:

Ricotta, about 11 ounces
Grated Parmesan cheese, less than 2 ounces
Beet greens, a handful
Flavor of nutmeg, and some of the spices preferred
Enough salt.
Eggs, 2

Pass the ricotta through a sieve and squeeze the watery part of it into a towel. Clean the beet greens from the bottom up and stew them without water over a low fire. Squeeze the water out of it. Make a mixture of all the ingredients. Place a spoonful of this mixture on some flour and roll it into a croquette-like shape. Boil the ravioli in saltless water and be careful that they do not break. Remove them from the water with a perforated spoon. Season the ravioli, or serve them as a side dish with a meat course.

61 — RAVIOLI IN ROMAGNA STYLE

Either because the climate of Romagna requires heavy food or because of odd habits, the Romagnoli dislike vegetables as much as we dislike the smoke of green wood in our eyes. Here is their recipe for ravioli, leaving out beet greens and spinach.

Ricotta, less than 6 ounces
Flour, less than 2 ounces
Grated Parmesan, 1½ ounces
Enough salt
Egg, one whole egg and one yolk

Make a compound of all these ingredients and place a spoonful of it on the flour already prepared and spread on a pastry board. Roll it, giving it any shape desired. Ordinarily, this compound suffices for about 1½ dozen ravioli.

Boil the ravioli in saltless water and season them with cheese and meat gravy. They may be served as a side dish with fricassee.

62 — RAVIOLI IN GENOESE STYLE

In this style ravioli is a misnomer, since real ravioli are not made with meat, nor are they enclosed in dough.

½ breast·of capon or of chicken
A whole brains of lamb and some sweet breads
A chicken liver

Place all these ingredients on the fire with a piece of butter. As soon as they become brown, add some meat gravy and allow them to cook. Remove the ingredients, dry and chop them all together with a slice of ham. Add a little boiled chopped spinach, grated Parmesan, flavor of nutmeg and 2 egg yolks.

Mix everything well and enclose the mixture in a pastry dough as for the cappelletti in Romagna style No. 6, or in any desired shape. This quantity ought to be enough for 60 ravioli. Cook them either in soup as a minestra or dry to be seasoned with cheese and butter, or with gravy.

63 — SPAGHETTI WITH ANCHOVIES

For a fast day minestra, this is an appetizing dish. Be sure to use spaghetti called "mezzani"; 12 ounces ought to be enough for 4 ordinary servings. 5 anchovies should be enough for the purpose. Remove the bones from the anchovies, wash them well and chop them. Place the anchovies on the fire with abundant olive oil and a pinch of pepper. Do not allow them to boil, but as they become hot, add 1½ ounces of butter, a little tomato gravy and remove them from the fire. Cook the spaghetti in water without much salt; they should not be too well done. Season them with the gravy just described.

64 — SPAGHETTI IN RUSTIC STYLE

The Romans considered garlic suitable for the poorest of their subjects, while King Alphonse of Castile hated it so much that he punished anyone who dared to smell of garlic at Court. The Egyptians were wiser, for they worshipped garlic as a Deity. Perhaps they had noticed its medicinal qualities. It is believed that garlic benefits hysterical people, helps urinal secretion, helps weak stomachs, facilitates digestion, and is an all around anti-epidemic remedy. However, when frying garlic, do not allow it to fry too much.

Some people, in banishing garlic as a plebeian flavor, miss its goodness. Its bad reputation as a strong odor is due to the habit of some peasants who eat raw garlic which is indeed strong. However, if used properly in preparing dishes, garlic flavors food with taste.

Try this simple recipe:

Chop finely two cloves of garlic and a good deal of parsley. Place a goodly measure of olive oil in a pan and set it on the fire with the garlic. As soon as it turns brown, cut six or seven fresh tomatoes into pieces and add them with a pinch of salt and pepper. When the tomatoes are well done, pass them through a sieve. This gravy should ordinarily suffice to season spaghetti for 4 persons. Cook the spaghetti in plenty of water; they should not be overdone; drain the water and season them with this gravy and Parmesan. Serve at once so that the spaghetti do not absorb the gravy before reaching the table.

65 — SPAGHETTI AND PEAS

This is a common enough minestra, but if well prepared it is very tasty. It is a dish that is welcome as an alternative to the customary liquid minestre with boiled meat.

Spaghetti, about 18 ounces
Shelled peas, about 18 ounces
Dry pork meat, a little over 2 ounces

Chop the dry pork meat, a fresh onion, a fresh clove of garlic, some celery and parsley. Place these chopped ingredients on the fire in olive oil, and as the mixture turns brown, throw in the peas together with a stick of anise, if available. Add a pinch of salt and pepper, and allow it to cook. Break the spaghetti into short pieces about 2 inches in length, boil them in salted water, drain well, and mix with the peas. Serve with Parmesan at side.

Ordinarily, this quantity is enough for 6 or 7 people.

66 — MINESTRA OF MASHED VEGETABLES

Take a bunch of beet greens, some spinach, a head of lettuce, and a leaf of curly cabbage. Discard the largest leaves from the beet greens, and cut all these vegetables into rather large pieces. Keep them in fresh water for a few hours.

Chop together ¼ of an onion, some parsley, celery, carrot, and a leaf of basil. Place all these ingredients in a pot and set it on the fire with a piece of butter. As soon as these chopped spices become brown, add the vegetables while still dripping. together with a sliced potato and some slices of fresh tomatoes. As soon as the vegetables have shrunk considerably, add enough hot water and let them cook till overdone. Pass them through a sieve, and in this fine vegetable gravy cook some rice, or use it to soak toasted bread, etc. Be sure to taste the gravy before adapting it to the various purposes, especially in adding butter to it. Serve such a minestra with Parmesan at the side, but do not serve it too dense because it would lose its delicate taste.

67 — CAPERS CROSTINI (Toast)

Pickled capers, less than 2 ounces
Pastry sugar (powdered sugar), less than 2 ounces
Raisins, about 1 ounce
Candied fruit, less than 1 ounce
Pine seeds, less than 1 ounce
Ham, less than 1 ounce

Chop the capers and the candied fruit thoroughly; wash the raisins in water; cut each pine seed into three parts lengthwise; cut the ham into small squares. Place a spoonful of flour and two spoonfuls of sugar in a small pan and set it on the fire. As soon as it turns a dark brown, pour a glass of water mixed with a thimbleful of vinegar on it. Allow it to boil till the tartness has dissolved. Then add all the ingredients together. Let them boil about ten minutes and taste them in order to adjust the bitter-sweet flavor peculiar to this antipasto. Vinegar is not always of the same strength, hence personal judgment must play its part in this work. Place this compound on small slices of bread, either fried in olive oil or plainly toasted. These crostini can be served cold as appetizers.

68 — CROSTINI WITH TARTUFI

(Truffles)

Cut the bread into diagonally-shaped slices, or into any other fancy shape desired and toast it. Butter the bread while hot and spread the truffles on it, prepared as described in No. 167.
Moisten them with left over gravy.

69 — CROSTINI WITH CHICKEN LIVER

Chop together a piece of shallot, or a piece of onion, a piece of fat ham, a few leaves of parsley, some celery and a carrot, and set everything on the fire in olive oil together with chicken liver. Add a piece of butter and a pinch of salt and pepper. Be careful that the spices are not out of proportion. When half cooked, remove the chicken liver dry; soak a few dry mushrooms and chop these two ingredients together finely. Replace the compound in the gravy from which the liver was removed; add a little soup to it, and let it cook. Before serving, thicken it with bread crumbs and flavor it with lemon rind. Remember that these crostini must be soft. It is not advisable to make the gravy too thick. The bread may be soaked in soup after toasting it, so that the desired softness will be acquired.

70 — A VARIETY OF CROSTINI

White bread is most suitable for these crostini. At any rate, use bread one day old. Cut it into square slices, $\frac{1}{4}$ inch thick, and remove the crust. Toast it and spread the following ingredients on it.:

* * *

Crostini with Anchovies: Wash and remove all bones from the anchovies. Chop them well; add a sufficient amount of butter and beat well with a knife blade till it is evenly mixed. Spread it on the toast.

* * *

Crostini of Caviar, Anchovies and Butter: The following proportions are in general use, but hey can be modified to suit individual tastes.

Butter, a little over 2 ounces
Caviar, 1½ ounces
Anchovies, less than 1 ounce

Mix well and work well till the compound has become smooth and ready for spreading on toast.

Crostini with Caviar: If the caviar is hard, soften it by exposing it to heat and adding some butter while working it with a long spoon. If oil is preferred to butter, be sure to squeeze in a few drops of lemon and mix well.

71 — CROSTINI OF CHICKEN LIVER AND ANCHOVIES

Chicken liver, 2 whole ones
Anchovy, 1

Cook the chicken liver in butter, gradually adding some soup; add a pinch of salt and pepper. Clean the anchovy, and as soon as the liver is done, chop both together. Replace the mixture in the gravy in which the liver was cooked; add another piece of butter; warm it on the fire without boiling it, and spread it on slices of fresh bread.

72 — CROSTINI FIORITI
(*Blossoming Crostini*)

These are easily prepared, beaufiful to look at, and quite tasty.

Cut clices of fine white bread, ¼ inch thick, into an oval shape. Spread fresh butter on them and place two or three leaves of parsley on them. Place slices of (filet) anchovies around the parsley, arranged in snake-like manner, and serve.

SALSE (*SAUCES*)

Of course the best sauce one can offer to one's guests is a gracious disposition and spontaneous cordiality. Brillat Savarin used to say: "To invite a friend means to safeguard his happiness during his stay at your house". Certainly one of the important elements in the duties of a host is the preparation of delicate sauces.

73 — SALSA VERDE (*Green Sauce*)

Chop together some pickled capers, one anchovy, a bit of onion and a little garlic. Beat this mixture with the blade of a knife till it is fine and smooth. Place it in the sauce dish. Add a goodly quantity of parsley and some basil; then dissolve the entire compound in olive oil and lemon juice. This sauce can be served with courses of boiled chicken, cold fish cuts or hard boiled eggs. If capers are not available, peppers will do as well.

74 — SAUCE OF CAPERS AND ANCHOVIES

This sauce is not for weak stomachs. It is ordinarily served with steak. Clean one anchovy and squeeze the vinegar from the pickled capers. Chop these two ingredients together and set them on the fire with olive oil just as long as it is necessary to heat them up without frying. Broil the steak, spread a little butter on it, and pour the sauce on the meat immediately after removing it from the griddle.

75 — SAUCE MAITRE D'HOTEL

This sauce is used for steak.
Chop a bit of parsley, and in order to take away

its acrid taste, put it into the corner of a napkin and press it out in fresh water. Make a mixture of butter, salt, pepper and lemon juice; put it on the fire and without letting it boil dip the steak into it when it is taken off the grate.

76 — MEATLESS SAUCE FOR SPAGHETTI

This sauce may not appear very attractive to the eyes but it will surely appeal to be palate. This is a recipe for five servings.

Spaghetti, about 18 ounces
Fresh mushrooms, a little over three ounces
Butter, 2½ ounces
Pine seeds, 2 ounces
Salted anchovies, 6
Fresh tomatoes, 7 or 8
¼ good-sized onion
Flour, 1 teaspoon

Place half of the butter in a pan and set it on the fire with the pine seeds. As soon as the pine seeds turn brown, remove them dry and grind them finely together with the flour. Chop the onion and place it in the pan from which the seeds were removed; and as it turns brown, add the tomatoes which have been cut into pieces. Add a pinch of salt and pepper. As soon as the tomatoes are done, pass them through a sieve. Set this sauce over the fire again together with the mushrooms, also finely sliced, the mashed pine seeds dissolved in a little water, and the rest of the butter.

Allow the sauce to boil half an hour while adding the necessary water to it. Finally dissolve the anchovies in a little of the sauce; place them on the fire to warm, and before they reach the boiling point, pour them into the sauce. Boil the spaghetti, strain them, and season them with the sauce and Parmesan cheese.

77 — WHITE SAUCE

This sauce is ordinarily served with asparagus or cauliflower.

Butter, 3 ounces
Flour, a spoonful
Vinegar, a spoonful
One egg yolk
Salt and pepper
Soup or water, as much as necessary

Set the flour on the fire in one half of the butter. As soon it turns to a light brown, pour the soup or water in, a little at a time, while stirring the sauce with a long spoon. Before the sauce has boiled too long add the rest of the butter and the vinegar. Remove it from the fire, immediately beat in the egg yolk and serve. Its thickness should equal that of heavy cream.

To assure enough of this sauce for a bunch of asparagus, use 2½ ounces of butter with a proportionate quantity of flour and vinegar.

78 — TOMATO SAUCE

In a town in Romagna an honest well-meaning priest was wont to stick his nose into everybody's business. Since tomatoes fit into every possible combination of food and since the good old priest was always present in other people's affairs, he was nicknamed *Don Pomodoro* to symbolize the inevitability of the presence of the tomato.

Chop together ¼ of an onion, a clove of garlic, a piece of celery 2 inches long, some basil and enough parsley. Place everything in a pot with sufficient olive oil, a pinch of salt and pepper, seven or eight sliced tomatoes, and set it on a slow fire. Stir often and when the tomato is well done, pass it through a sieve.

This sauce can be used in many ways. We will see how as we go on with our recipes. For the present, let me say that it can be used with boiled meat, to season spaghetti together with cheese and butter, or with risotto (rice).

79 — MAYONNAISE SAUCE

This is one of the most delicate sauces. It is excellent with boiled fish. Place two fresh egg yolks in a deep dish; beat them for a while and pour in, gradually, almost drop by drop, six or seven spoonfuls of olive oil. Add the juice of one lemon and beat everything well for twenty minutes. A well-made mayonnaise sauce must have the density and the appearance of cream. Then season it with salt and a goodly measure of white pepper.

80 — PIQUANT SAUCE I.

Chop finely together two spoonfuls of pickled capers, two anchovies and a bit of parsley. Place this mixture in a sauce dish with a goodly pinch of pepper and plenty of oil. If it is not sufficiently pickled, add some vinegar to it and some lemon juice. Serve with boiled fish.

81 — PIQUANT SAUCE II.

Chop finely together a little onion, some parsley, a leaf of basil, a piece of lean ham and some pickled capers. Place this mixture in fine olive oil and set it on the fire. Allow it to boil slowly and as soon as the onion becomes brown, add a few spoonfuls of soup. Allow it to boil a little longer and remove it from the fire. Add 2 chopped anchovies and a little lemon juice. This sauce is ordinarily served with steaks, hard-boiled eggs, and cutlets.

82 — YELLOW SAUCE FOR BOILED FISH

The following proportions are ordinarily sufficient for a steak or a fish of about one pound. Set less than one ounce of butter and a heaped spoonful of flour on the fire in a small pot. As soon as the flour has become light brown, pour in two ladlefuls of the soup of the fish you are to dress, and let it boil. As soon as the boiling flour ceases to thicken, remove it from the fire. Add two spoonfuls of oil and one egg yolk and mix well. Finally, add the juice of half a lemon, a pinch of salt and a good measure of pepper. Allow the sauce to cool off and pour it on the fish to be served. Some parsley leaves in their natural state are ordinarily set alongside the fish. The density of this sauce should be similar to that of cream so that it adheres to the fish. If the fish is preferred warm, serve the sauce hot.

83 — CAPER SAUCE FOR BOILED FISH

Butter, less than 2 ounces
Pickled capers, less than 2 ounces
Flour, a heaped spoonful
Salt, pepper and vinegar

This quantity is sufficient to dress a little more than one pound of fish. Boil the fish, and while preparing the sauce, leave it in its own water so that it is warm at the time of serving.

Set the flour with half of the butter on the fire; mix well and as it takes on color, add the rest of the butter. Allow it to boil for a while and pour in a ladleful of fish water. Add the capers (half finely chopped, and the other half whole). Flavor it with a few drops of vinegar and taste it so as to adjust it to individual preference. The sauce should be as dense as cream. Place the fish on a platter while warm, pour the sauce on it, add some parsley, and serve.

84 — SAUCE IN GENOESE STYLE
FOR STEWED FISH

Pine seeds, about 1½ ounces
Pickled capers, ½ ounce
Salted anchovies, one
Hard-boiled egg yolks, one
Pickled, pitless olives, three
Half a clove of garlic
A good deal of parsley, stalks included
A piece of crustless bread, the size of an egg, soaked in vinegar
A pinch of salt and pepper

First chop the garlic and the parsley finely, then place these in a mortar and add the rest of the ingredients to them. Beat thoroughly till the contents is reduced to a paste-like compound, and pass it through a sieve. Dilute it with two ounces of oil and some drops of vinegar and adjust its taste to your palate.

This amount is sufficient to dress about 22 ounces of fish.

85 — THE SAUCE OF THE POPE

The name of this sauce is of uncertain derivation. It is hardly possible that it took its name from the Vatican pope, because though tasty, it is not a heavenly delicacy. It is a good sauce for chopped cutlets.

Squeeze the vinegar from a goodly pinch of pickled capers; add an equal amount of sweetened pitless olives and chop them together finely. Set some chopped onions and about one ounce of butter on the fire and as they take on color, add some water gradually, till the onions are well done. Pour in the mixture of capers and olives and allow it to boil a while. Add a few drops of vinegar, a pinch of flour, and another piece of butter. As a last touch, add a chopped anchovy without any further boiling, and serve.

86 — TRUFFLE SAUCE

Chop together a small piece of onion, half a clove of garlic and some parsley. Set it on the fire with less than 1 ounce of butter, and as it takes on color, pour in 1/1 glass of marsala wine, or plain white wine. in which a spoonful of flour has been previously mixed. Salt it; add some pepper and some agreeable spice. Stir often with a spoon. As soon as the flour has blended with the rest of the ingredients, add a little soup and then enough thinly-sliced truffles. Let the sauce remain on the fire a few moments and serve it as dressing for milk-fed veal cutlets, or any boiled or roast meat.

87 — BALSAMELLA SAUCE

Put a tablespoon of flour and a piece of butter as large as an egg on the fire. Mix it to melt the flour and the butter together and when it begins to turn the color of hazelnut pour a pint of milk on it little by little, stirring constantly until the liquid has condensed into a milky cream. If it is too thick add water; if too liquid put it on the fire again with another piece of butter dipped in flour.

A good balsamella sauce and a meat sauce chopped up properly are the basis of first-rate cooking.

88 — GREEN PEPPER SAUCE

Open some large green peppers, remove the seeds, clean them and cut each one into four or five slices. Place these slices in a pan with a little oil and heat them enough to facilitate the removal of the skin. After skinning the peppers, lay them aside. Set some chopped garlic in oil and a piece of butter on the fire. As soon as the garlic takes on color, add the peppers. Salt them, add some tomato sauce, and allow it to boil for a while. To retain the piquancy of the peppers, do not cook them too long.

89 — POACHED EGGS

Open the eggs while the water is boiling and drop them into it from a low height. As soon as the egg white solidifies and the yolk is steady, remove the eggs with a perforated spoon, and put them in a platter. Add salt, pepper, butter and cheese. Il preferred, the eggs may be dressed with tomato sauce, green sauce No. 73, or a sauce made especially by melting an anchovy in warm butter and adding some chopped pickled capers to it.

90 — OMELET IN SANDALS (*Zoccoli*)

This omelet requires special though simple handling. Cut slices of ham into pieces as large as a 25 cent coin and set them on the fire in the omelet pan with some butter. Pour in the beaten eggs; add a little salt after they have cooked a while. As soon as the eggs solidify, fold half of the omelet over the other half, add another piece of butter, and wait till it is done.

91 — ONION OMELET

One large, white onion should be used for this omelet. Cut the onion into slices one inch long and soak it in fresh water for one hour. Dry the onion in a canvas towel. Prepare the pan with lard or oil. Place the onion on the fire, and as it takes on color, add some salt. Pour in the beaten eggs and cook the omelet in the usual way.

92 — SPINACH OMELET

Boil the spinach in water and as soon as it is removed from the fire, place it in cold water. Squeeze the water from the spinach, chop it roughly, and set it on the fire in a pan with a piece of butter. Add a pinch of salt and pepper. Turn the spinach often. As soon as the butter has been absorbed by the spinach, add a little salt and throw in the beaten eggs. When the omelet has browned sufficiently on one side, turn it over and replace it on the fire with an added piece of butter. If preferred, a pinch of Parmesan may be added to the eggs.

For a four-egg omelet, 7 ounces of raw spinach and 1½ ounces of butter is the right proportion of ingredients.

93 — FRIZZLED OMELET AS A SIDE DISH

Stew a small bunch of spinach and pass it through a sieve. Beat two eggs, add enough salt and pepper and mix them with enough spinach to make the compound green. Moisten a pan with oil, set it on the fire, and when hot, pour part of the egg in it, moving the pan energetically with a circular movement so as to keep the omelet as thin as paper. When well dried, remove it to a platter. Repeat the operation with the rest of the eggs and then place these omelets together and cut them into fine, noodle-like strips. Place a piece of butter in a pan and fry these strips, adding some Parmesan cheese to them. Serve these frizzled curls as a side dish to a fricassee or a similar dish. Besides being an attractive side dish, this omelet will mystify the guests by its strangeness.

94 — FOIL DOUGH FOR PASTRY

The main problem about this dough is that when puffing it, it must foliate well and at the same time remain light and taut. It is somewhat difficult to prepare, but we shall try our best to succeed.

Fine white flour, 7 ounces
Butter, 6 ounces

In the Winter, use warm water, but not too hot, in mixing the dough. Add enough salt, a spoonful of brandy and a piece of butter taken from the above quantity. Knead all this into a loaf of medium softness, working it first with the hand for about half an hour, and then throwing it vehemently and repeatedly against the pastry board. Give the loaf a rectangular shape; fold it into a canvas towel and let it rest a while. In the meantime, work up the butter on the board with wet hands till it has become like a fine even paste, and shape it into a loaf. Place the butter loaf into cold water. When the flour loaf has rested long enough, remove the butter from the water, dry it well with a towel and cover it with flour.

Flatten the dough as much as necessary so as to enfold the butter loaf in it. Place the butter in the middle; and, stretching the sides of the dough, enclose it by bringing these up, with wet fingers, and forming a loaf again. Be sure that the dough covers the butter well and that no openings are left. Begin to flatten the dough with the hand; then apply the rolling pin. While the dough is being flattened, watch that the butter does not spurt out. If this happens, stop it with flour and continue to roll it till the dough is reasonably flat. Then fold the dough into three layers and again roll it into thinner sheets. Repeat the operation six times, allowing the dough to rest for ten minutes each time. When the dough is about to be rolled for the seventh time, fold it into two layers and roll it into the desired thinness. Except for the last folding, the dough should be given a rectangular form; that is to say, three times longer than wide.

It is advisable, when possible, to roll the dough on a marble board instead of a pastry board. The coldness of the marble as well as its smoothness facilitates the process. In the Summer, use ice to harden the butter in the dough by placing the ice in a canvas towel and laying it on the dough whenever necessary.

With this pastry dough are prepared the following: vol-au-vent, French pastry made with marmalades of fruit preserves, as well as pies, and all kinds of sweet breads. Stuffed meat cookies with minced lamb liver or sweet-breads can also be made from this dough. At any rate, any pastry or cookies made with this dough should be sprayed with egg-yolk on the surface only, because if sprayed on the edges the egg-yolk will prevent the cookies or pies from puffing up.

95 — SEMI-FOIL DOUGH

Half as much butter as flour should be used, in addition to a small piece of butter placed in the dough. See preceeding recipe for instructions.

96 — LIQUID DOUGH FOR FRITTERS
(*Pastella*)

Flour, 3 ounces
Fine olive oil, a tablespoonful
Eggs, one
Sufficient salt
Cold water, as much as necessary

Mix the flour with the egg yolk and the rest of the ingredients. Pour the water slowly, little by little, so that the dough will not become too thin. Work it well with a long spoon and let it rest for a few hours. When about to use the dough, beat the egg white and add it. This dough has many uses, but it is used mostly for vegetable fritters.

97 — STUFFING FOR CHICKEN

Lean, milk-fed veal, 3 ounces
A piece of breast of veal
The entrails of the chicken.

Lean pork can be used in place of the milk-fed veal and breast of veal. The breast of turkey serves the purpose as well.

Cut the meat with a piece of chopped onion or scallion, some parsley, celery, carrots and butter. Add a pinch of salt, pepper and other spices dressed, and pour sufficient soup on it. Remove the meat from the pan, dry. Now clean the entrails, add some sliced ham, some mushrooms, and chop these ingredients finely. Throw a spoonful of bread crumbs into the gravy left in the pan and mix well. Add a dash of

Parmesan and two eggs and stuff the chicken. Sew it up well and cook it in the style preferred. If the stuffed chicken is boiled, you will get excellent soup, but be sure to cut it open carefully, so that the stuffing will not be crushed when served in slices.

98 — MEAT STUFFING FOR FOIL-DOUGH PIES

(Dumplings or Foil-Dough Dumplings)

This stuffing may be made with milk-fed veal (very well done), with chicken liver or sweet-bread. Sweet-bread is a real delicacy for the purpose. Whatever meat is used, an excellent flavor to add is that of truffles when in season.

If sweet-bread is chosen, set this on the fire with a piece of butter, add salt and pepper; and, as it colors, add sauce No. 4, and let it cook. Cut the sweet-bread into pieces as large as peas, add a bit of salted tongue and some ham (also cut into small pieces), a pinch of Parmesan cheese and the flavor of nutmeg. Be careful to balance the proportion of ingredients, and let the compound get cold.

There are two ways of enclosing the stuffing in foil dough No. 94, but in both cases, the size of the disc-like pieces should be about three inches in diameter. The first method is that of placing the stuffing in raw dough and cooking them together. The second method is that of cooking the foil dough first and then enclosing the stuffing in it. In the first case, place the stuffing in the middle of the disc, wet the edge with a wet finger, place another disc on it and cook the dumplings. The second method is more suitable for people who must prepare a large dinner and will find it convenient to cook the foil dough the day before, in the following way: place one disc on top of another without the stuffing, but before placing the upper disc on the lower one, take a ring of tin, or other metal, and imprint a circlet the size of a quarter on it. When boiled, the space marked by the circlet will puff up, thus leaving a hollow space inside. With the point of a knife-blade, remove the circlet cover, place the stuffing into the hollowed space and place the little cover on it again. Remember to gild the dough with egg-yolk before cooking it.

99 — FRIED STUFFED DOUGH

Cut disc-like pieces of foil dough of a diameter of two inches, as in No. 94, possibly indented at the edge. Place the stuffing of the preceding recipe in the middle of the disc, cover it with another disc of the same dough; wet the dough on the edge so as to assure adhesion; fry and serve while hot.

100 — FRIED APPLES

Remove the core of some large apples with a core carver, skin the apples and cut them into slices of about a quarter of an inch. Place these slices in flour dough No. 96. Il preferred, add some anise flavor, and fry them. Sprinkle them with powdered sugar, and serve while hot.

101 — FRY OF RICOTTA

Ricotta, 7½ ounces
Flour, 1½ ounces
Eggs, 2
Sugar, 2 spoonfuls
Flavor of lemon rind
A pinch of salt and a spoonful of brandy

Be sure that the ricotta is not sour. Mix these ingredients well into a compound and let it rest for several hours before frying. In this way the mixture will get hard so that it can be shaped into balls as large as nuts. After these balls have been fried dash some powdered sugar on them, and serve them as a side dish while hot.

102 — FRIED FENNEL

Cut the fennel into slices, remove the hard leaves, and boil it in salted water. Dry it thoroughly, cover it with flour, place it in flour dough No. 96, and fry.

103 — FRIED PEACHES

Cut peaches that are not overripe into slices of ¼ inch, place them in flour dough No. 96 and fry them. When fried dash powdered sugar on them, and serve. The skin need not be removed.

104 — FRIED PORK LIVER

It is admitted by many that the real taste and flavor of this liver is enjoyed only when the liver is fried in its natural state in virgin lard, mixed with common sweet-bread of the same liver. Cut the liver into small slices and fry it in a pan with some ot its own fat; add salt and pepper and while still hot, squeeze the juice of a lemon on them to diminish the lardy taste. If preferred, the liver slices may be covered with flour before frying them.

105 — MIXED FRY IN BOLOGNESE STYLE

This fry could more appropriately be called "fine croquettes." Take a piece of lean milk-fed veal which has been overcooked, a small brain which has been boiled in meat sauce, and a slice of lean and fat ham. Chop everything in a mortar very finely. Add the yolk of an egg or the whole egg, according to the quantity of the meat, and a bit of balsamella sauce No. 87. Put the mixture on the fire and stirring it constantly let the egg cook. Finally add grated Parmesan cheese, flavor of nutmeg, very finely chopped truffles, and pour it in a plate. When it is cold make little round meat balls, the size of a nut, and pass them in flour. Pass them in some beaten eggs and in very fine bread crumbs, repeating the process twice. Fry them.

106 — FRY IN ROMAN STYLE I.

Chop a little onion and set it on the fire with a piece of butter. As soon as it colors, place a piece of lean milk-fed veal in it, add a pinch of salt and pepper, and allow the meat to brown. Add some marsala wine, and let it cook well.

Mash the meat in a mortar. If it is too hard moisten it with the gravy left in the pan or with a little soup. Finally, add an egg-yolk. This mixture should be rather hard.

Cut some rather thick wafers into small squares. Beat a whole egg and the egg white left from the yolk used previously. Dip the wafer squares, one by one, in the egg, and place each one on some stale grated bread. Add to each wafer a small amount of the mashed compound. Now dip as many wafer squares as before, into the egg, one by one, and place grated stale bread on one side. With the second supply of wafers cover the stuffing, attaching them to the lower wafer. Dash on more grated bread if necessary, and lay each square aside separately.

Fry these squares, either in oil or lard, and serve them as a side dish. The ordinary proportion for this dish is about seven ounces of meat for twenty stuffed squares.

107 — FRY IN ROMAN STYLE II.

This fry should be made whenever there is a breast of boiled chicken to spare. The following are the ingredients for five servings:

Breast of broiled chicken, about 2 ounces
Salted tongue, 1½ ounces
Ham, a little over one ounce
Parmesan cheese, a spoonful
Either a small truffle, or the flavor of nutmeg

Remove the skin from the chicken breast and

cut it into small squares. Do likewise with the tongue, the ham and the truffle.

Make a gravy with:

Milk, less than ½ pint
Butter, 1 ounce
Flour, 1 ounce

When this gravy (balsamella) is cooked, add the ingredients to it and let it cool off. Prepare the wafers as in the previous recipe. Fry them in the same way and serve them as a side dish.

108 — RICE FRITTERS I.

Milk, a little over a pint
Rice, 3 ounces
Flour, 3 ounces
Raisins, less than 2 ounces
Pine seeds, cut crosswise and in half, ½ ounce
Eggs, 2
Butter, a goodly square
Sugar, two spoonfuls
Rum, a spoonful
Flavor of lemon rind
Yeast, as much as the size of a nut
A pinch of salt

Place some of the flour, about one ounce, on the pastry board, make a hole in the middle of the heap of flour and liquify the yeast into it with milk. Knead it into a dense loaf, making an incision on it so that you can easily see when the yeast has risen.

Cook the rice in part of the milk till it is considerably dense, but do not allow it to stick to the pot. When the rice is almost cooked, add the pine seeds, raisins, butter, sugar, salt and the lemon rind. Allow the rice to cook together with these ingredients, and remove it from the fire. When cool, add the risen yeast loaf, the eggs, the remainder of the flour (2 ounces), and the rum. Mix all these well and replace the pot on a low fire. When the mixture has risen, make ready for the usual frying and place the compound in the sizzling pan, spoonful by spoonful so that the fritters may be large and light. Sprinkle sugar on them while still hot, and serve at once.

109 — RICE FRITTERS II.

These are simpler than the ones described in the previous recipe.

Cook 3 ounces of rice in a little over a pint of milk, adding to it a square of butter, a pinch of salt, a teaspoonful of sugar and the flavor of lemon rind. Allow it to cool and add a spoonful of rum, three egg yolks, and less than 2 ounces of flour. Mix well and let it rest for several hours. When about to fry as described above, beat the three egg whites well and add them gradually to the compound. Fry the rice by spoonfuls as for the other recipe; sugar the fritters while hot, and serve at once.

110 — FARINA FRITTERS

Milk, one pint
Farina, over 4 ounces
Butter, a goodly square
Rum, a spoonful
Flavor of lemon rind
Salt, to individual taste
Eggs, 3

Cook the farina in milk, salt it when cooked; let it cool off and then add the eggs and rum. Fry this compound in small separate quantities in oil or lard; dash sugar over the fritters while hot, and serve.

This amount ordinarily suffices for four or five servings.

111 — FRIED ARTICHOKE

This is a simple fry and yet very few people seem to do it properly. However, we are going to fry the artichokes in the manner of Tuscany, which is the best way I know of.

Remove all the hard leaves from the artichoke; cut the tips of the edible leaves; clean the bottom of the artichokes, and cut them into two equal parts. Then cut these two parts into slices so as to cut eight or ten slices from each artichoke. As you cut these slices, throw them into cold water; when they have become quite cool, remove them and squeeze out the water. Cover them with flour immediately so that the flour remains attached.

Beat the white of an egg; mix the yolk with it and add salt. Place the artichoke slices in a sieve and shake off the superfluous flour. Dip the slices in the egg and let them rest for a while so that the egg may adhere well. Place butter in a pot, wait till is sizzles, and place the artichokes in it. As soon as the artichoke slices take on a golden hue, remove them from the fire and serve them at once with slices of lemon at the side. If you wish to keep the artichoke white, use oil when frying it and squeeze half a lemon on it when placing it in the water.

112 — FRIED YOUNG SQUASH I.

This is a favorite dish with almost anyone, but aside from that, it is suitable as a side dish with many fried food courses.

Cut young squash into slices two inches long and a quarter of an inch wide. Wash them well and remove the seeds from the core. Salt them sufficiently and let them rest for two hours. Squeeze the water from the squash, cover it with flour and place it in a sieve so as to shake off the superfluous flour. As the oil sizzles in the pan, throw the squash in. When fried well, remove the squash from the fire with a perforated spoon so that the slices do not break.

113 — FRIED YOUNG SQUASH II.

This should be even more palatable than the one described in the preceding recipe.

Take a little more than a handful of squash remove the skin, split each squash into two parts lengthwise and remove the seeds from the core. Cut them into slices two inches long and $1/4$ inch wide; salt them and let them rest for an hour. Squeeze the water from the slices with the hands. Cover them with flour, one by one, and place them in a sieve. Fry in a large quantity of oil till they have taken on a golden color, and serve.

114 — DOUGHNUTS (*Ciambelline*)

Put a casserole containing 6 oz. of water, a piece of butter as large as a nut, two teaspoons of sugar, and a pinch of salt on the fire. When it is boiling, dissolve 4 oz. of flour in it, throwing it in all at once, so that no lumps are formed, and start stirring immediately. Take it from the fire quickly and while it is still boiling, break an egg into the liquid and mix it vigorously until it is well dissolved. When the mixture is cold, add two more eggs at intervals, stirring continually until the ladle drags after it a thin veil of dough. Add the vanilla extract, spread some flour on the pastry-board and pour the dough on it. Start working the dough with the hands covered with flour, and roll it up so that it is covered with enough flour to become consistent, but is still soft.

Divide the dough into 16 or 18 parts forming little balls slightly larger than nuts; make a hole in the middle of each ball by pressing it with the point of a finger against the pastry-board and turning it on itself. Turn the balls over and do the same on the opposite side, so that the hole becomes large and even, and the balls take on the appearance of doughnuts. Put a wide pot of water on the fire, and when the water is very hot, but not boiling, throw in the doughnuts three or four at a time. If they stick to the bottom, lift them with a perforated spoon, turn them; and when they come to the top, take them out and place them on a piece of cloth. With the point of a knife make an incision on each one, on both the exterior and interior sides, so that the swelling in the pan will be more even.

Fry them in much grease on a low fire, shaking the pan often; if they have been made well they will grow to an extraordinary volume, remaining dry,

Cover them with powdered sugar when still warm and serve.

115 — CRESCIONI (*A sort of Spinach Pie*)

There is no reason why these spinach pies should be called crescioni. At any rate, let us describe how they are made, and let it go at that. Cook the spinach in the usual way, without water, and when done squeeze the water from it thoroughly. Chop together a clove of garlic and some parsley and place this in a pan with sufficient oil, together with the spinach. Allow it to stew and add some raisins and boiled grape juice. Use sugar if no boiled grape juice is on hand. When the spinach has been prepared, cut pie-crust dough into circle-like pieces, about three inches in diameter. Place enough spinach in the center of each disc and fold it into a half moon. Fry in abundant oil, and serve as side dish.

116 — CROQUETTES

Almost any meat pick-ups may be used. Prepare the croquettes in the manner of the meat balls described in No. 193, without using the raisins and the nuts. If preferred, flavor with garlic and parsley. As to the shape, roll them into a spool-like form, as is usual when they are fried.

117 — SWEET-BREAD CROQUETTES

Place 5 ounces of sweet-breads in a pan together with either gravy or some chopped onion and butter.

Add salt and pepper, flavor with nutmeg and allow to cook. Add two spoonfuls of the gravy described in No. 107, an egg yolk and a dash of Parmesan cheese. Now take the sweet-bread compound, spoon by spoon, and throw it on grated bread or cracker-dust, and roll it into spool-like croquettes. Dip them into beaten egg, then into cracker-dust again, and fry. If preferred, small squares of ham may be added to the compound. The above amount of sweet-bread is ordinarily sufficient for ten or twelve croquettes, which can be added to other fried delicacies to make an excellent mixed fry.

118 — RICE CROQUETTES

Milk, a little over a pint
Rice, 3 ounces
Butter, ⅔ ounce
Crated Parmesan cheese, ⅔ ounce
Eggs, 2

Cook the rice in milk, and when half done, add the butter and salt. Let the rice absorb the milk entirely and remove it from the fire. Add the Parmesan and one egg, and mix well. When cold, remove the rice from the pot by spoonfuls, and, mixing each spoonful with cracker-dust, shape it into a spool-like form till twelve croquettes have been made. Beat the other egg, and dip each croquette into it. Roll them in cracker-dust and fry the entire quantity. These croquettes may be served either as a separate dish or with other fried dishes.

119 — MIXED RICE CROQUETTES

Follow the preceding recipe, but when the rice is well done, add the entrails and liver of a chicken, and let everything boil in gravy and butter. If preferred, instead of gravy, a piece of chopped onion, lends an agreeable taste. Remember to cook the chicken entrails and liver before chopping and adding them to the rice.

120 — RICE PEARS

Rice, 3 ounces
Milk, a pint or a little more
Butter, a goodly square
Parmesan, a generous pinch
Eggs, one

Boil the rice in milk. When the rice is half done, add the butter, and when it is well done, salt it. Remove it from the fire. As it becomes cools, break the egg into it and add the Parmesan. Cook two chicken livers and two lamb sweet-breads, flavoring them with nutmeg. Cut these into pieces the size of a peanut; add some chopped ham, truffles and mushrooms to them. This combination gives the dish a very delicate taste.

Now take a funnel having an opening of 1½ inches and a sharp cone less than ¾ inch in length. Smear it with butter and spray some craker-dust on it. Fill half of it with rice, then add two or three pieces of the meat compound and complete the filling with rice. The rice will acquire a pear-like shape as soon as it is removed from the funnel by blowing into it. Repeat the operation till all the rice is used up. Gild each rice pear with beaten egg yolk and cracker dust. Fry in the usual way and serve.

121 — LAMB MEAT IN OMELET

Cut some loin lamb into pieces and fry it in virgin lard. Since this meat is rather fat, not much lard is needed. When the lamb is half done, add a pinch of salt and pepper, and when entirely done, throw in four or five beaten eggs. Mix well and do not allow the eggs to harden too much.

122 — GILT FOWL I.

Remove the insides of a spring chicken, cut off the head and feet, wash it well and place it in boiling water for one minute. Remove it and cut it into pieces at the joints only. Cover it with flour, dash on a pinch of salt and pepper, and then pour two beaten eggs on it. Let it rest for half an hour, and cover the pieces with grated bread. Repeat the operation twice, and broil the chicken in the following manner:

Place sufficient oil or virgin lard in a pan or a pie dish and when it begins to sizzle, place the chicken in it. Let it brown on both sides, over a low fire, so that the heat will penetrate evenly to the interior. Serve it with lemon at the side while still hot. Note that the wings of turkey, when boiled and cut into pieces, are very delicious if cooked in this manner.

123 — GILT FOWL II.

Prepare the spring chicken as described in the preceding recipe, and cut it into smaller pieces. Cover the pieces with flour, immerse them in salted beaten eggs; fry them in a pan, add a pinch of salt and pepper, and serve with slices of lemon at side.

124 — CHICKEN IN HUNTER STYLE

Cut a large onion into pieces and leave it in cold water for half an hour; dry it thoroughly, place it in a pan with oil or virgin lard. Place it over the fire, and when cooked, remove the onion and set it aside. Cut a spring chicken into pieces and fry it in the fat from which the onion was removed. As soon as it browns, add the onion, season it with salt and pepper, and pour a glass of red wine over it. Let it boil for five minutes, place it in a dish, and add some tomato sauce. This is a dish for strong stomachs.

125 — FRIED CHICKEN WITH TOMATOES

The people of various countries fry food with the kind of fat which is most abundant as a native product. In Tuscany, oil is preferred; in Lombardy, butter is the customary thing; and in Emilia, lard is the favorite fat. The Emilian lard is excellent, and the chicken cooked in it tastes very good.

The compiler of this book prefers lard for frying because it lends a special fragrance to meats.

Cut the chicken into small pieces and place it in a pan with sufficient lard; add some salt and pepper.

When it is done, drain the lard from the chicken and add several pieces of tomatoes, after having removed all the seeds carefully. Stir often so as to prevent sticking, and when the tomatoes are well done, serve the dish.

126 — LIVER FRIED WITH WHITE WINE

Wine in cooking is not of the author's preference but since success in good living depends on one's capacity in conciliating one's individual taste with that of others, I suggest the continuance of this good habit. At any rate, be sure to choose the best of white wine any time you wish to prepare this dish.

Cut the liver into fine slices and fry it in sufficient oil and butter. Beat a spoonful of flour in white wine, preferably muscatel, and set it aside. When the liver is about done, add the liquid and allow it to cook. When cooked, add salt and pepper.

127 — FRIED CREAM I.

Starch, 3 ounces
Sugar, ¾ ounce
Eggs, two
Milk, a little over one pint
Flavor of vanilla or lemon rind

Beat the eggs and sugar them well. Grind the starch into powder and add it to the eggs. Grate the lemon rind and add it also. Finally, pour the milk in gradually, and add the butter. Place this mixture on the fire. Stir continually till it has condensed. When it has thickened enough, add the salt, and place it in a dish, spreading it evenly into a layer ½ inch thick.

When cold, cut the cream into almond-like pieces, dip each piece in beaten egg and grated bread, and fry it in virgin lard or oil. Serve it while hot as a side dish with other fried dishes.

128 — FRIED CREAM II.

Starch, 3 ounces
Sugar, 1 ounce
Butter, ¾ ounce
Milk, 1 pint
Eggs, two
Flavor of lemon rind
Salt, a pinch

Keep the mixture on the fire till the flour has lost its rawness. Follow the preceding recipe for the rest of the preparation. This quantity is ordinarily enough for eight servings when used as a side dish.

129 — HEAD OF LAMB

I know of two other styles besides boiling, to cook head of lamb. It may either be fried or roasted. For frying, see recipe No. 199, while for roasting, use your own judgement, since it is the same as any other roast.

130 — LAMB LIVER AND CHITTERLINGS IN BOLOGNESE STYLE

Cut the liver into thin slices, and the chitterlings into pieces. Place everything on the fire with lard.

When the liver and chitterlings are done, drain all the fat from it. Add a piece of butter. Continue to fry gradually and pour on tomato sauce or tomato paste. diluted in soup. Season with salt and pepper, and serve.

131 — LAMB FRIED IN BOLOGNESE STYLE

The best part of lamb for frying is loin, but shoulder or neck is also excellent. Cut the lamb into small pieces and fry it as described in the preceding recipe.

132 — FRIED RABBIT

The meat of rabbit is not very nutritious, nor is it very tasty. However, the taste can be improved by cooking it with appropriate seasoning. It is quite agreeable. and it is a meat more digestible than lamb. It is the meat for the poor man whose earnings prevent him from buying choice beef.

The best way to cook rabbit is to fry it in the style described for lamb in the preceding recipe. Some say that boiled rabbit makes excellent soup. Remember that Confucius speaks of the rabbit as fitting as a gift to the Gods, and I dare say that if such is the esteem in which it was held by the Chinese sage, it ought not to be out of place on our table.

133 — STUFFED CUTLETS

Have the butcher cut the meat thinly and uniformly. The right meat is either milk - fed veal or breasts of chicken and turkey. If veal is chosen, about six ounces of boneless meat will suffice.

Make a gravy with 2½ ounces of flour, one ounce of butter, and less than half a pint of milk. When cooked, salt it and remove it from the fire. Break an egg into it, and while mixing it, add a pinch of Parmesan. Let it cook off.

Cut the meat for cutlets into pieces as large as a silver dollar and spread the gravy on both sides. Now cover the cutlet with craker dust and fry it in oil or lard over a low fire. It will be a delicately flavored dish.

134 — STUFFED BREAD

Take one or two chicken livers, some sweetbread and, if available, a chicken or turkey gizzard. The gizzard should be partly boiled first and the tissue removed.

Chop all the meat and put it on the fire with a sauce made of onion, ham and butter; season with a small amount of salt, pepper, nutmeg or spices. When it begins to sizzle pour in a level teaspoon of flour, mix, and add meat sauce or broth. Boil, and pour in a beaten egg a little at a time, and stirring constantly, let the mixture thicken. Take it off the fire, add a pinch of Parmesan cheese, and pour it into a plate.

Take a stale roll, cut it into slices half an inch thick, remove the crust and cut it into squares. Pour the mixture on the bread, so that only one side is covered with it. Half an hour before frying, spread flour on this side and scatter the bread on a platter.

Pour on some beaten egg so that the bread becomes wet and the sauce is covered. Throw the bread into a frying pan on the side covered with the sauce.

135 — MILK-FED VEAL CUTLET

Cut some lean milk-fed veal into very thin slices, and beat each piece with the back of a knife blade without breaking it into separate bits. Place a pan with oil and butter on the fire and add a few sage leaves. When these have fried for a short while, add the cutlets. Add a pinch of salt and pepper. Allow the cutlets to fry on a strong fire for five or six minutes. and remove them. Squeeze a slice of lemon on the cutlets and serve. This is a delicious dish for lunch.

136 — FRY A LA GARISENDA

This is a fried dish to keep in mind, for it is very tasty.

Remove the crust from some stale bread and cut it into squares of about one inch. Be sure that the squares are all of equal size. On each square place first, a slice of ham, then a slice of truffle, and finally a slice of Gruyere cheese. Cover this stuffing with another square of bread and press them well together. Be sure to cut all the ingredients thinly, so as to make very thin squares.

Now that the ingredients are prepared, soak each square in cold milk and wait till the milk is absorbed. Dip each square into beaten egg, then cover it with cracker dust. Repeat the operation twice, so that the egg closes the edge of the square. Fry these squares in lard or oil and serve them as a side dish with other fried courses.

137 — BRAINS, SWEET-BREADS, TENDER HEADS, ETC.

For all these fried dishes, make use of the sauce for fried meats described in recipe No. 107.

SIDE DISHES
138 — CRESENTINE (*Garlic Toast*)

The old folks say that since garlic is a good worm killer, this toast is especially good for children. Toast both sides of some slices of bread. While hot, rub them with a clove of garlic. Add some salt, pepper, oil, vinegar and sugar.

139 — DONZELLINE (*Fritters*)
STUFFED WITH SALTED ANCHOVIES

A recipe for six. It is appropriate as a side dish with fish courses for lunch.

Flour, about 9 ounces
Butter, 1 ounce
Milk, as much as necessary
Salt, a pinch
Salted anchovies, 4

Knead the flour, butter, milk and salt into a loaf, neither very soft nor too hard, and place it in a pan to rise. Let it rest for a while. In the meantime, clean the anchovies by removing the backbone lengthwise. Cut them into little square pieces. Cut the loaf in half. Place the pieces of anchovies on one half of loaf; cover them with the other half so as to make the dough stick together, and apply the rolling pin. Roll the dough into a thin foil. Cut this foil dough into almond-shaped pieces and fry them in oil.

140 — AROMATIC DONZELLINE

A recipe for three people:

Flour, 3 ounces
Oil, 2 spoonfuls
White wine, or marsale wine, 2 spoonfuls
Sage leaves, five
Sufficient salt

Chop the sage leaves finely and knead all the other ingredients into a rather soft dough. Work it well and roll it to a thinness equal to that of a silver dollar coin. Spray some flour on it and cut it into almond-shaped pieces. Fry either in oil or lard. Some prefer this dish with fresh figs and ham.

141 — SEMOLINO (Farina) GNOCCHI

Milk, less than one pint
Semolino (Farina), 3 ounces
Butter, less than 2 ounces
Parmesan cheese, 1½ ounces
Eggs, two
Salt, as much as necessary

Cook the semolino in milk. When about to remove it from the fire, salt it, add the butter and half of the Parmesan. While still warm, add the eggs and mix well. Spread it either on a pastry board or on a flat pan, in a thickeness of ½ inch and allow it to cool off. Cut it into almond-like pieces. Place these in a flat pan, or a pie dish, arranging them in layers, placing small pieces of butter between them, and dashing some Parmesan cheese on each layer. No cheese is necessary on the surface. Place the gnocchi in the oven, let them brown, and serve them while hot.

142 — GNOCCHI IN ROMAN STYLE

I have modified these gnocchi somewhat, because it seems to me that if prepared as described below, they are very palatable.

Flour, 5 ounces
Butter, 1½ ounces
Gruyere cheese, ¾ ounce
Parmesan cheese, ¾ ounce
Milk, 1 pint
Eggs, two

The saying goes that the number of diners should not be less than the number of races, nor any bigger than the family of the muses. If they are as many as the muses, the thing to do is to double up the dose of ingredients.

Mix the flour with the eggs and milk in a pot, pouring the milk in a little at a time, so as to allow the flour to absorb it gradually. Cut the Gruyere cheese into small pieces and add. Place the mixture on the fire and keep stirring it. When the flour has become thick through the cooking process, add half of the butter. Allow it to cool off. Using a dish that can stand oven heat, place the compound in it in small pieces, as for the yellow flour gnocchi. As the dish is gradually filled, add the rest of the butter pieces together with grated Parmesan. Do not dash Parmesan on the surface because it becomes bitter when heated. Brown the gnocchi in the oven and serve while hot

143 — POLENTA OF YELLOW FLOUR AND SAUSAGES

Prepare a rather soft polenta with corn flour, spread it on a board, in a thickness of ½ inch, and cut it into almond-like pieces.

Set a pot containing a few pieces of sausage and a little water on the fire; allow the sausage to stew well and remove the skin. Cut the sausage into small bits and add either tomato sauce or tomato paste.

Place the polenta pieces in layers into a pie dish. On each layer spread some Parmesan cheese, sausage, and here and there a piece of butter. Place the polenta in the oven, let it heat and serve it while hot. This is an appropriate dish for lunch.

144 — SEASONED POLENTA (*Pasticciata*)

Cook some thick polenta of yellow flour in milk. Salt it and spread it on a pastry-board in a thickness of about 2 inches. When it is cold, cut it into almond-shaped pieces of half inch. Prepare a sauce as for the macaroni No. 52 and some balsamella No. 87. Then arrange the polenta in a metal tray as follows: Spread some Parmesan cheese on the bottom of the tray, add a layer of polenta, season it with cheese and the two sauces; add another layer of polenta similarly seasoned. Continue the process till all the polenta is used up. Add little pats of butter here and there.

Put the tray in a country-oven and let the polenta brown. Serve as a side dish while hot.

145 — MACARONI WITH PANGRATTATO
(*Grated Bread*)

If it is true that Alexander Dumas senior said that the English people live on roast beef and pudding; the Dutch on baked meat, potato and cheese; the Germans on sauerkraut and pig's knuckles; the Spaniards on chick peas, chocolate and rancid salt pork; it is no wonder that I harp on Macaroni, which is the favorite Italian dish.

Here is another style of macaroni:

Long macaroni, 9 ounces
Flour, ½ ounce
Butter, 2 ounces
Gruyere cheese, 2 ounces
Parmesan cheese, 1½ ounces
Milk, a little over a pint
Sufficient grated cheese

If the macaroni are preferred richer, add enough of the above ingredients to suit the taste.

Cook the macaroni till they are half done, salt them and drain the water from them. Place half of the butter and flour in a pot on the fire and stir continually. As it takes on color, pour the milk in, little by little, and allow it to boil for ten minutes. Add the balsamella, the macaroni and the grated Gruyere cheese and lower the fire so as to allow the macaroni to boil very slowly till the milk has been absorbed. Add the rest of the butter and the grated Parmesan. Now place the whole thing into a baking dish and cover it with pangrattato (grated bread). Place the macaroni in the oven and allow them to bake till they are browned; serve as a side dish with meat courses.

146 — MACARONI
WITH BALSAMELLA GRAVY

Cook some long macaroni in salt water, but remove them from the water while still hard. Place the macaroni on the fire with a piece of butter. As soon as they have absorbed the butter, add sufficient milk and let them finish cooking over a low fire.

Prepare the balsamella as in No. 87, and when it has cooled, add an egg yolk. Add the balsamella to the macaroni together with sufficient grated Parmesan cheese. This style of macaroni is ordinarily served as a side dish with boiled beef or veal fricassee. When served with meat, allow the macaroni to brown in the oven, or simply bake them. Be sure not to serve them very dry.

147 — DRESSED LAMB CHOPS

Use only meat of very fine quality. Loosen the bones from the chops. Flatten the chops evenly and cook them sautè style in butter. Add a pinch of salt and pepper and set them aside.

Prepare a balsamella. Add to it a small piece of ham and salted tongue, a pinch of Parmesan cheese, flavor of nutmeg, a sliced truffle or some mushrooms, and set it aside to cool.

Now prepare sufficient foil dough as described in No. 94. Dip the chops into the balsamella and cover them, one at a time, with the foil dough, leaving the bone uncovered. Close the edge of the dough tightly and gild it with beaten egg yolk. Place chops, standing up, leaning against the wall of a deep cake dish and bake them in the oven. Wrap the bone of the chops in waxed tissue paper and serve hot.

148 — STUFFED ROLLS

Grate the rough crust of rolls lightly, carve a cone the size of a quarter out of each roll. Remove as much crumb as possible from the roll, but see to it that the walls are left rather thick. Soak the rolls, both inside and outside, in boiling milk. Soak the cone likewise and replace it in the roll so as to form a solid outer surface again. Fry the rolls in either lard or oil, placing the side of the opening of the cone against the bottom of the pan so that it will adhere well to the rest of the roll. When fried, remove the cone with a sharp knife, and stuff the empty space with chopped liver, breast of chicken, sweet-breads, etc., after having cooked these ingredients in succulent gravy. Cover the stuffing and serve while hot.

149 — CORN PUDDING I.

If you like corn flour, you can prepare a tasty pudding with little effort. Children, especially, enjoy this food.

Select corn flour, not too finely ground. Place as much flour as necessary in any suitable vessel, salt it and mix it with boiling water. When no vestige of dry flour is visible, add raisins in just proportion. Place sufficient virgin lard in a cake dish, and as soon as it begins to sizzle, throw the millet in. Spread it evenly with a long spoon; smear the surface with more virgin lard, and add some rosemary leaves. Either bake it or cook it between two fires. When it is brown, remove it from the cake dish. If preferred, fritters may be made with the same millet, but in that case, do not use rosemary leaves.

150 — CORN PUDDING II.

This is a more delicate dish than the preceding one.

Corn flour, 10 ounces
Raisins, 3½ ounces
Fat, 1½ ounces
Pine seeds, 1 ounce

Remove the seeds from the raisins and cut the Pine seeds in two, crosswise. Smear a cake dish with fat and spread flour on it. As for the rest, see preceding recipe.

151 — EGGS AND SAUSAGE

Eggs and sausage make a good combination. The same can be said for any dry meat cut into small pieces, though one is wont to consider such a dish a rugged type of food.

If the sausage is fresh, cut it into two slices lengthwise, and cook it in a pot without any fat. If dry sausage is used, cut it into small slices and remove the gut or skin. As soon as the sausage is cooked, break the eggs into it and serve it as soon as these are done. The ordinary proportion is one egg for each sausage. When the sausage is too lean, cook it with a bit of lard or butter.

152 — SAUSAGE AND GRAPES

This is a very ordinary dish, but many people may find the bitter-sweet of the grapes very tasty.

With the point of a fork make holes in the sausage and place it in chunks in a pot containing either lard or butter. When done, add the grapes, one by one, allow it to boil till it has been reduced to half the original size, and serve.

If the sausage is desired plainly cooked, just place it in a pot and let it cook over a low fire with a few drops of water.

153 — RICE AS A SIDE DISH

Whenever boiled chicken or capon is served, do not neglet a side dish of rice, for it is very appropriate. In order to save on soup, boil the rice half way in water; then finish cooking it in chicken soup. Allow it to thicken, and when nearly done, add a piece of butter and flavor it with a little Parmesan. When done, and about to be removed from the fire, add one beaten egg for every 7 ounces of rice.

If, instead of chicken, milk-fed stracotto (over-boiled veal), or any other meat dish is served with rice as a side dish, add two spoonfuls of mashed spinach. This will give a delicate green rice. The appearance of the rice may be improved by placing it in a double boiler for the last part of its cooking, without allowing it to harden too much.

154 — ARTICHOKES COOKED IN A BAKING PAN

This is a Tuscan dish, relatively inexpensive and quite good. It may be served at lunch either as a side dish or as antipasto.

Prepare the artichokes in the manner described in No. 111. When the superfluous flour has been shaken off from the artichokes, place them in a baking pan as soon as the oil begins to sizzle. Beat up enough eggs and salt them. Add a pinch of salt to the artichokes and as soon as they become brown on both sides, pour in the beaten eggs. Do not allow them to cook too much.

155 — TORTINO OF TOMATO

(Tomato Pie)

Make a fricassee with a piece of garlic, some parsley, oil, salt and pepper, and add some sliced tomatoes. Allow it to cook till the tomato is condensed quite well. Pass the tomato through a fine sieve and replace it on a low fire. Beat up sufficient eggs and add them with a dash of Parmesan. Mix well. As soon as the eggs are done, place them in a dish and surround them with crostini, toasted pieces of bread, almond-shaped, and fried in butter or lard. A leaf of calamint adds a fine flavor.

156 — MAYONNAISE SALAD

Some people prepare this salad with boiled chicken; others with any kind of roasted meat; but fish is preferable, especially if it is of fine quality, as for instance, grayling, peeled crab, lobster or sturgeon. Some people make use of pigeon meat also, but the following recipe is quite good, though very simple.

Cut some Romain lettuce into strips and mix it with beet roots, boiled potatoes (sliced), some anchovies (cleaned of backbone and each cut into four parts), and some chopped boiled fish. Add a few capers and two or three olives. Season everything with salt, oil and a good deal of vinegar. Mix very well so as to allow the seasoning to seep through, and make a heap of the salad in a dish.

Prepare a mayonnaise sauce as described in No. 79, sufficient for seven or eight persons, but instead of pepper, use mustard as a piquant. Add a few drops of vinegar to the lemon. Smear the surface of the salad with this mayonnaise sauce and add more slices of beet roots and potatoes in a pattern that appeals to the eye. If you have the form, make a butter flower and place it at the top.

157 — BOOK-LIKE PIZZA

The credit for this fine pizza goes to a lady who willingly offered her knowledge to an eager learner.

It is true I had to try at least twice before I mastered the art of preparing it, but I am happy to jot down this recipe for those whose taste is discriminating.

Enough flour to be mixed with 2 eggs, a pinch of salt, and three spoonfuls of cognac, or brandy, is all that is required. Mix all these ingredients and knead the whole into a loaf which is not too hard; then roll it into a thin foil dough. When this is done, melt 2|3 ounce of butter and smear the foil dough with it. Fold it so as to place the buttered part inside, and make a roll 6 inches wide. Now cut this in half, lengthwise, and then crosswise, so as to obtain several rectangular pieces. Press the back, or the uncut part of each piece and fry in abundant oil or virgin lard. Dash powered sugar on these pieces and serve. If you succeed in preparing this pizza in the proper form, you will see that it opens up like pages of book.

This amount is ordinarily enough for four persons.

158 — STRACOTTO OF VEAL

Stracotto of veal for seasoning macaroni or a risotto is the meat preferred by bourgeois families. It is quite an idea, for it serves a double purpose. It is a main dish, as well as a second course at the same time. Do not sacrifice the quality to the quantity of the soup in preparing the stracotto, and when possible, substitute olive oil for dry pork meat.

Lean veal meat, including bone, 18 ounces
Dry pork meat, less than 2 ounces
Butter, more than one ounce
One fourth of a large onion
A small carrot
∴ few pieces of celery

Cut the last three items into large pieces and the dry meat into dice-like pieces.

Place everything on the fire together and add salt and pepper. Turn the meat often, and when brown on both sides, spread a pinch of flour on it. Add some tomato sauce or diluted tomato paste and allow it to cook in water, added to the meat little by little, as necessary.

Remember that the flour gives color and consistency to the gravy, but do not allow it to burn, because this would give the gravy an undesiderable taste and a dark color. Strain the gravy through a sieve and flavor it with slices of mushrooms.

Boil the macaroni in salted water, drain the water, season them with stracotto gravy; add a pinch of Parmesan, a piece of butter and place the macaroni in the oven for a short time. Serve with Parmesan at side. As for the stracotto meat, serve it with vegetables.

If rice is preferred, boil it half way in water, then add stracotto gravy, a piece of butter, and, when about to remove the rice from the fire, a pinch of Parmesan.

159 — ODD STRACOTTO

To a piece of boneless veal weighing about 1½ lbs., add about three ounces of sliced salt pork. Add salt and pepper and bind it all together with a string. Place it on the fire in a pan, covered with water. Add two sage leaves, a few leaves of rosemary and half a clove of garlic. If the meat is tender, use less water. When the water has boiled down, add a teaspoonful of flour and let it take on color. Add a piece of butter, then pour in a ladleluf of soup and $1/4$ of a glass of marsala wine. Strain the gravy without squeezing it too much and pour it over the meat when serving.

160 — FRICANDO (*Special Pot Roast*)

To a piece of milk-fed veal, cut from the leg, add a slice of ham; then tie it well together with a string. Add very little salt. Make a little bunch with slices of onion, two cloves, a sliced carrot, celery and parsley, and place it in a pot together with the meat and a piece of butter. Allow the meat to brown and add a ladleful of soup. Let it cook slowly over a low fire. When the meat is cooked, remove the onion and the fat from it, and let the gravy, boil till it is concentrated and resembles a gelatine. This gravy is to be served scparately when serving the Fricando meat.

161 — FRICASSE

Fricassee can be made with breast or leg of milk-fed vcal, lamb or chicken. Let us begin with breast of veal. The same recipe with equal proportions will serve for the other kinds of meat.

Breast of milk-fed veal, 18 ounces
Butter, less than 2 ounces
Flour, a spoonful
Warm water, (not boiling), ½ pint
Egg yolks, two
Half a lemon
A small bunch of aromatic herbs

Cut the breast of veal, bones included. Place a pan with half of the butter on the fire. When the butter begins to melt, add the flour and stir well till it has taken on a light tan. Add the warm water little by little, and immerse the small bunch of aromatic herbs in it. Aromatic herbs may consist of long slices of onion, carrots, parsley, celery and basil.

When the water boils, add the meat, the rest of the butter, a pinch of salt and white pepper. Place a sheet of wax paper over the pan and cover it tightly. Allow it to boil slowly over a low fire. When it has cooked for about 2|3 of the time allotted to it, remove the aromatic herbs and add about 6 ounces of sliced fresh mushrooms. If no fresh mushrooms are available, use dry ones after soaking them in water, for they serve the purpose as well.

When about to serve the fricassee, remove it from the fire, and pour in the beaten egg yolks gradually while constantly stirring it with a long spoon. Finally squeeze in the lemon and serve while hot.

If it is a chicken fricassee, cut the chicken at the joints, remove the breast and feet, and follow the same method for the rest. The fricassee is a delicate dish, and it will satisfy the taste of those who are not in the habit of eating strongly spiced food.

162 — CIBREO OR FRICASSEE

Cibreo is a delicate dish. It is good for convalescing people, or for ladies with lazy stomachs. Ingredients for one person are:

4 chicken livers
4 cocks' combs
7 chicken kidneys
1 egg yolk
Lemon juice
Flour

Remove the skin from the cocks' combs in hot water and cut each into two or three pieces. Cut the chicken livers into two pieces. Place some butter in a pot on the fire; add the cocks's combs, later the liver, and, finally the kidneys. Season with a pinch of salt and pepper; add a little broth, if necessary, and let it cook slowly.

Now place an egg yolk in a small pan. Add half a teaspoon of flour, some lemon juice and boiling broth, while beating the egg yolk. When the fricassee is cooked, pour in the beaten egg yolk, and, if necessary, a little more broth, so that it may be rather loose. Serve while hot.

163 — STUFFED BONELESS CHICKEN

The following is the simplest method for removing bones from a chicken. Clip off the wing tips about half way. Cut off the neck and head, the ends of the wings, and the feet from the joints of the legs down. Without removing the entrails, open the chicken in the back, from the wings down to the end of the back-bone. With a sharp knife working from inside, first remove the wing bones, thoroughly clean of meat. Next, always from the inside, remove the hip bones and those of the legs. Then, continuing to carve the external bones of the fowl, free it entirely from the bones. The entrails must also be removed in the same way. Now remove the breast or sternum, and turn the legs and wings inside out. Clean the meat of all tendons and put the limbs back in place. Now the boneless chicken is ready for stuffing.

Prepare the stuffing with:

10 ounces of milk-fed veal
3 eggs yolks
⅔ ounce of ham
⅔ ounce of salted tongue
A goodly pinch of Parmesan cheese
Flavor of nutmeg

Chop the veal finely and then beat it with a pestle in a mortar. Soak a slice of bread in soup and add it to the veal. Add the Parmesan, the egg yolks, the salt and pepper; also the flavor of nutmeg. Cut the ham and tongue into small squares an add. Mix all ingredients well and stuff the chicken. Sew the opening together, wrap the fowl in a thin cloth and tie it well. Allow it to boil in water on a low fire. for two hours. Remove the cloth and brown the chicken in butter. Then allow it to boil for a while in a gravy prepared as follows:

Chop the bones removed from the chicken, the neck and the head and add a few pieces of dry pork meat. Place all this and some butter, onion, celery and carrot in pan on the fire. When this has been fried for a short time, add a sufficient amount of the chicken soup made from the stuffed chicken. Before serving, remove the stitches from the chicken.

164 — CHICKEN IN PEASANT STYLE

Tie a few leaves of rosemary, and a clove of garlic (split into four pieces) to a pullet. Make a fricassee of salt pork, salt and pepper, and place it on the fire with the pullet. When it is browned all around add a few slices of tomatoes and wait till they are well done. Add some broth or water and allow the whole thing to boil over a low fire.

Now fry separately, either in oil or lard, a few slices of raw potatoes, then add them to the gravy in which the fowl is cooking, and serve. If a more delicate taste is preferred, use butter instead of salt pork.

165 — CHICKEN WITH MARSALA WINE

Cut the chicken into large pieces and place it in a pan on the fire together with a fricassee made of onion and a piece of butter. Add a pinch of salt and pepper. When the chicken is browned all around, add sufficient broth and allow it to cook. Strain the gravy; remove all the fatty part, if necessary, and place the chicken on the fire again with the gravy, adding a little marsala wine. As soon as it comes to boiling point, remove and serve.

166 — CHICKEN WITH EGG SAUCE

Cut a spring chicken into pieces and place it on the fire with less than 2 ounces of butter. Add salt and pepper. When fried, spread a pinch of flour on it. Let it take on color; add enough soup and allow it to cook. Remove the chicken from the gravy and keep it warm in the oven while beating up egg yolk. Squeeze a few drops of lemon into the egg yolk and pour it into the gravy. Mix well. When about to serve the chicken, pour this sauce on it.

167 — CHICKEN BREASTS A LA SAUTE

This is a palatable dish as well as an economic one. If cooked as described, a single breast of capon is sufficient for four portions.

Cut the breasts into thin slices, almost as thin as paper. Trim these pieces as nicely as possible. Add a pinch of salt and pepper and place them in beaten egg. Let them remain in the egg for one hour. Remove and cover the slices of breasts with cracker dust. If the meat is preferred plain, just fry the slices and serve with lemon. Otherwise, prepare a sauce in the following manner:

Take a small pan and barely cover the bottom with oil. Put in some sliced mushrooms, spread a pinch of cracker dust or grated stale bread on them. Repeat the operation three or four times. Add some oil, salt and pepper, some butter, all in small quantities, so as not to give the food a fatty taste. Now place this small pot on the fire, and as it comes to a boiling point, add a small ladleful of meat soup and a few drops of lemon. Remove from fire quickly, add it to the breasts already cooked, and serve.

168 — WILD DUCK

In buying a wild duck, open its beak and look at its tongue. If the tongue it too dry, it is a sign that the bird is not freshly killed. Some people prefer to remove the wild odor from the fowl by washing it in vinegar before cooking it; others suggest washing it in boiling water; however, since the odor comes from the coccygeal gland, which is located at the end of the backbone, the odor will disappear when the gland is removed. This gland contains a viscous yellowish liquid, found in all water birds.

Remove the entrails, but set aside the heart and kidneys. Cut off the head and remove the skin from the neck, and then bend the neck into the breast.

Now make a fricassee in the following manner: If the duck weighs more than 2 pounds, chop finely one ounce of ham together with some celery parsley, carrot and a quarter of a big onion. Place this mixture on the fire in a pot containing sufficient oil and lay the duck into it, flat. Add a pinch of salt and pepper. Allow it to brown all around and add sufficient water. Let it cook slowly.

It is customary to prepare a side dish of black cabbage for this main dish, and here is the simplest way of cooking it: Boil the black cabbage, then let it take flavor in the gravy in which the wild duck has been cooked. Serve the cabbage with the duck.

169 — DOMESTICATED DUCK

Prepare this bird as in the preceding recipe. Place it on the fire with a similar ham fricassee. When the duck has browned all around, add some tomato sauce or diluted tomato paste. Let it cook while pouring the necessary soup or water on it. Strain the gravy and remove the fat from it. Then replace it in the pot with the duck and a piece of butter.

With this gravy and some Parmesan cheese you can season a minestra of large noodles, while you serve the duck with a side dish of vegetables as a second course.

170 — PIGEON RAGOUT

Dress the pigeons with sage leaves. Place some slices of ham in a pot, place pigeons on the top of the ham: add some oil, pepper and very little salt. Allow them to brown and add a piece of butter, and let them cook in a little soup. When about to remove them from the fire, squeeze in a lemon. Serve the pigeons on toast, spreading the gravy in which they were cooked on them. Sour grapes, when in season, may be used instead of lemon.

171 — PIGEON COOKED IN ENGLISH STYLE

For this tasty dish you need:

One large young pigeon
Milk-fed veal or chicken breast, 3½ ounces
Thinly sliced ham 2½ ounces
Thinly sliced tongue, ⅔ ounce
Butter ⅔ ounce
Half a glass of fatless soup
Hard boiled egg, one

Discard both the head and the feet of the pigeon and cut the rest into pieces (at all the joints). Cut the veal or chicken breast into slices and flatten them with the blade of a large knife. Cut the ham and tongue into slices ½ inch wide and cut the egg into eight parts.

Use either a metal pan or a porcelain dish which can stand a strong fire, and arrange the ingredients in layers in the following order: One half of the pigeon and veal ;one half of the ham and tongue; spread bits of butter here and there; add four pieces of egg. Sprinkle on some salt, pepper and some spices. Repeat the operation with the remainder of the ingredients till they are all used up. Finally add the cold soup which is floating on the edge of the dish, and the larger part of it will remain there after the pigeon is cooked.

Now knead a crust with which to cover the pigeon, as follows:

Flour, about 6 ounces
Butter, 1½ ounces
Wine alcohol, a spoonful
Sugar, a spoonful
Juice of a slice of lemon
One egg yolk
Sufficient salt

Mix the flour with all these ingredients. If necessary, add enough luke warm water so that the dough will be soft. Work the dough by throwing it repeatedly against the board; then let it rest a while and roll it into the thickness of a pie crust dough. Fold it into four or five layers, and again roll it to the thinness of a pie crust with a grooved rolling pin. Now cover the meat dish with this crust dough and gild the surface of it with beaten egg yolk. Bake in a country oven and serve while hot.

172 — MANICARETTO OF PIGEONS

(*Ragout*)

Cut the pigeons into large pieces, preferably at the joints and place them on the fire in a pot together with a slice of ham, a small piece of butter and a small bunch of aromatic herbs. Add sufficient salt and some pepper. As the pigeons begin to dry or when they are half done, add some pieces of sweet-bread; sliced fresh mushrooms, or dry soaked mushrooms. If truffles are available, add these when the pigeons are almost done. Now add sufficient soup. It two pigeons are used, pour half a glass of hot white wine, kept ready for the purpose, on the meat. Boil slowly, add a little flour and a piece of butter so as to give consistency to the gravy. When about to serve the pigeons remove the ham and the bunch of aromatic herbs and squeeze in the juice of a lemon. Be sure to boil the sweet-bread before adding it to the pigeon.

This is a good recipe for cooking pullets as well.

173 — TIMBALE OF PIGEONS

Make a fricassee with ham, onion, celery, carrot and butter, and put it on the fire together with one or two pigeons. Add giblets of the pigeons and also some chicken giblets if available. Season them with salt and pepper and, when the pigeons are browned, add some broth to cook them. Strain the sauce formed by the pigeons and throw some partly cooked macaroni into it. Keep the macaroni near the fire, turning them from time to time. Prepare some balsamella sauce. Break the pigeons at the joints and remove the bones. Cut the giblets into large pieces.

When the macaroni have absorbed the sauce, season them with Parmesan cheese, pieces of butter, slices of lean and fat ham, nutmeg, slices of truffles or dried mushrooms. Finally add the balsamella and mix.

Smear a casserole with butter, line it with foil dough, pour in the mixture, cover it with the same dough, and cook it in the oven. Serve while hot.

10 oz. of macaroni and 2 pigeons are sufficient for a timbale for ten or twelve persons.

174 — THRUSHES WITH OLIVES

Thrushes and all other edible birds can be cooked according to recipe No 170 because they are very savory. At any rate, you may slightly change the taste by adding pickled olives, when half cooked. Some people prefer not to remove the pit from the olives, but I suggest that this be removed. Cut the olives into small strips so as to allow each strips to form a hollow cylindrical spiral olive.

175 — STEWED BLACKBIRDS

Blackbirds are somewhat tough, and therefore should be prepared in the following manner:

For six blackbirds chop together ¼ of a large onion and a little more than one ounce of ham. Place it on the fire with ⅔ oz. of butter, three or four thin slices of ham and a few drops of juniper juice. Place the whole blackbirds on top; do not open them. Dress with sage leaves and sprinkle on salt and pepper. When the birds have absorbed the flavor of the onion fricassee and are evenly browned, pour in some dry white wine, in all ⅔ of a pint. Cover the pot with a four fold sheet of paper and place a heavy metal cover on it, so that the paper adheres well. Boil on slow fire till done. Serve the birds with their own gravy.

176 — BIRDS IN SALMI

Broil the birds till they are half done on a griddle. Baste with salted oil. Remove from griddle. If the birds happen to be thrushes or another small type, leave them whole; if they are big birds, cut them into four pieces. Remove the heads and mash them in a mortar together with some small broiled bird. Place them on the fire in a small pot with a fricassee consisting of butter, a small piece of ham, meat gravy or soup, some Madeira or Marsala wine in a quantity equal to that of the soup, a chopped scallion; one or two juniper berries for thrushes, or a leaf or two of laurel for any other kind of bird. Add sufficient salt and some pepper. Let the gravy boil half an hour. Pass through a fine sieve; place in a pot with the broiled birds. Allow to boil slowly till well done and serve on toast.

177 — RABBIT STEW

Later on, I shall describe how to make rabbit pie or roast rabbit. However, if you wish to make this stew bitter-sweet, you may apply recipe No. 178 in preparing the following.

If the rabbit is to be cooked, cut the rabbit into pieces. Make a fricassee by chopping together finely one medium-sized onion, two cloves of garlic, a goodly-sized piece of celery and several leaves of rosemary. Place this on the fire with a small piece of butter, two spoonfuls of oil and four or five small slices of ham. After this fricassee has cooked for five minutes throw in the rabbit pieces, add sufficient salt, pepper and other spices. When brown, add half a glass of white wine, then a handful of either fresh mushrooms or soaked dry mushrooms ad let it cook slowly in soup and tomato paste. Before serving, make sure to taste it and add butter, if necessary.

178 — BITTER-SWEET WILD BOAR

Is seems to me that the only wild boar to cook in this style is one with at least ½ inch of fat on its skin, for the fat of this wild hog is not nauseating. In fact, it is rather palatable.

The following proportions and the recipe are for about 2½ lbs. of wild boar:

Chop together finely one half onion, half a large carrot, two sprigs of celery, a little parsley and one ounce of ham. Place this fricassee in a pot with oil, salt and pepper. Put in the wild-boar meat and let it cook. When the meat is evenly browned. drain the greater part of the fat off, sprinkle a pinch of flour on it and cook it in warm water added gradually, a little at a time.

In the meantime, with the following ingredients, prepare the bitter-sweet in a glass and add it to the meat.

Dry grapes, 1½ ounces
Chocolate, 1 ounce
Pine seeds, 1 ounce
Candied fruit, in pieces, ⅔ ounce
Sugar, less than 2 ounces
Sufficient vinegar

At the beginning add little vinegar, for it is advisable to add more later. Make sure that the bitter-sweet cooks long enough with the meat to be well absorbed. It is advisable to prepare the dish a day ahead, for it will taste better. If a simpler bitter-sweet is preferred, use only sugar and vinegar.

179 — WILD BOAR BETWEEN TWO FIRES

Keep the meat in the solution described for rabbit in No. 311. Remove it and dry it in a towel and proceed to prepare it as follows:

Place three of four thin slices of lardon at the

bottom of a pot; on top of them place the wild boar meat; salt and pepper it and add a whole onion, a bunch of aromatic herbs, a piece of butter and for about 2½ lbs. of meat, half a glass of white wine. Place three or four slices of lardon on top of the meat and cover it with a sheet of paper smeared with butter. Make sure that the paper adheres well. Cook it between two fires (preferably with charcoal fire). When it begins to dry up, add enough soup to keep it moist. When cooked, strain the gravy without pressing; remove the fat from the gravy and add it to the meat when serving.

180 — BITTER-SWEET TONGUE

A milk- fed veal tongue is to be preferred for this dish. Remove the skin as follows: Heat a platter; place it on the tongue; as you remove the platter, peel off the skin. Repeat the operation till the tongue is clean. Boil the tongue till half done. For the rest of the instructions, see No. 178 and use the water in which the tongue was boiled.

181 — FRIED KIDNEYS

Take either one big kidney or several small ones and remove the fat, thus removing that disagreable odor which is often associated with kidney. Cut it crosswise into thin slices, place it in a pot, salt it, and pour in enough boiling water to cover it. When the water becomes cold, drain it and dry the slices in a canvas towel. Place them in a pan with a piece of butter; turn them often, and when they have fried five minutes, sprinkle a thin pinch of flour on them. Add salt and pepper. Boil half a glass of white wine and add. Allow the kidneys to remain on the fire a little longer, and when about to remove them, add another piece of butter, a few sprigs of chopped parsley and a little soup, if necessary. Be sure not to leave them on the fire too long, else they become hard. Marsala wine or champagne are very good substitutes for white wine.

182 — KIDNEY IN FLORENTINE STYLE

Open and remove the fat from the kidney as in preceding recipe. Cut it in half, either crosswise or lengthwise, and cook as follows: Place a pot with a proportionate piece of butter on the fire. As it begins to sizzle, add the kidney. Allow it to cook a while and remove it from the fire. Add salt, some pepper and a few sprigs of chopped parsley. Mix the kidney well in this sauce, and after a few hours cover it with grated bread and cook it in the same pot or on a griddle.

183 — ROAST OF LEG OR OF SHOULDER OF MUTTON I.

The best way to cook this meat is as follows: The shoulder may serve as a guide for the leg. The mutton should be of a fine brand and quite fat. Assuming that three or four lbs. of meat are to be cooked, remove the bone, put a few slices of lardon in the meat, add some salt and pepper, botch it and tie it into an oblong shape. Place the meat in a roaster with

1½ounces of butter and allow it to brown. Then add the following ingredients: Some pick-ups of smoked ham skin, the usual bunch of celery, parsley and carrot, a medium-sized onion, the bone previously removed, any fresh meat pick-ups on hand, a glass of soup, two spoonfuls of brandy, enough cold water to reach, but not to cover, the surface of the mutton.

Cover well and allow to boil on a slow fire till done. Four hours or more are necessary if the meat is not tender. Remove it from the fire, strain the gravy and remove the fat from it. Serve mutton without this broth.

As a side dish for mutton, it is customary to make use of carrots, turnips or mashed beans. Cook the carrots in the same pot with the meat, cut them into slices and serve. If turnips are used, be sure they are not sour. Turnips are usually cut into pieces, dipped in flour, browned in butter, and boiled in the gravy from the mutton. If beans are used, cook them in water first and then allow them to take on flavor in the mutton gravy.

184 — ROAST OF LEG OR OF SHOULDER OF MUTTON II.

This is the simpler recipe, and when no vegetable side dish is required, it is to be preferred to the preceding one. Remove the bone from the shoulder, put a few slices of lardon sprinkled with salt and pepper into it. Salt the meat, botch it and tie it strongly. Place it on the fire with 1½ ounces of butter, half an onion and some cloves of garlic. Allow it to brown and remove it from the fire. Pour in a glass of water, or, preferably, soup, a spoonful of brandy, the usual little bunch of aromatic herbs, and a few slices of tomato.

Allow the contents to boil over a slow fire for three hours and see to it that pot is tightly covered with a double sheet of paper under the metal lid. Turn the meat often. When done, remove the onion and strain the gravy, remove the fat and serve the gravy along with the meat.

Do not allow the meat to overcook because this hinders slicing. Leg of mutton can be made in the same way.

185 — BEEF A LA BRACE
(Burning cinders)

This is the French *boeuf braise*. Buy a goodly piece of lean and tender beef, weighing over 1 pound. Put 1½ ounces of sliced lardon into the meat, roll it and tie it with a piece of clean string. Sprinkle salt and pepper on it. Chop ¼ of a medium onion, half a carrot, and a full-length sprig of celery into a fricassee.

Place this in a pot with one ounce of butter, and the meat on top. As this fricassee is cooking and the fat is being absorbed, add a few drops of cold water at two times. When the fricassee is well done and the meat is browned, add two ladlefuls of warm water, cover the pot with a double sheet of paper and allow it to boil slowly till the meat is well done. Strain the gravy, remove the fat and replace it on the fire with a small piece of butter, to give the meat a delicate flavor. The fat will improve the gravy, in which a side dish of spinach, Bruxelles cabbage, carrot, fennel, etc., may be cooked

186 — SCALOPPINE, LIVORNESE STYLE
(*Scallops*)

Why this meat dish was named scaloppine and why so christened at Leghorn, I cannot say. At any rate, flatten some slices of boneless meat well, and in order to preserve the tenderness of the meat, place it in a pan with a piece of butter. When the butter has been absorbed, moisten the meat with a spoonful of soup. Allow it to cook well, add sufficient salt and some pepper, sprinkle on some flour, and flavor with a few drops of Marsala wine and some chopped parsley.

187 — SCALOPPINE OF CHOPPED MEAT

Any meat from a large animal will do. Remove all tendons and chop well. Season with salt, pepper and grated Parmesan. Add the flavor of some spices if preferred. Mix well and shape the meat into a ball. Now sprinkle some grated bread on a board, place the meat in the center, sprinkle more grated bread on the meat, and flatten it with the rolling pin. Loosen it often from the board to prevent sticking, and roll it into the thickness of a silver dollar. Cut into square pieces, 3x3 inches, and fry it in butter in a frying pan. When browned, add some tomato sauce, or tomato paste diluted in stock soup or water, and serve.

If preferred, the meat may be flattened with the

hand. Meat pick-ups are a good ingredient to mix with the raw meat in preparing this meat dish

188 — SCALOPPINE, GENOESE STYLE

Cut a little more than a pound of lean veal into slices. Chop one quarter of an onion of medium size and place it in a pan with oil and a piece of butter. Place some slices of veal on this, one layer on top of another. Sprinkle with salt and pepper, and place it on the fire without stirring, to prevent shrivelling. When browned on the lower side, add a teaspoon of flour, and a little later, a pinch of parsley chopped together with a clove of garlic. Pour in ¼ of a wine-glass of white wine. Separate the veal slices from each other; soak them well in the gravy so that they absorb it. Add warm water, some tomato sauce and allow them to cook slowly. Serve on toast with a good deal of gravy. If preferred, serve them with a side dish of rice, boiled in plain water but lightly seasoned with a piece of butter, Parmesan cheese and some gravy.

189 — STUFFED BRACIUOLINE
(Stuffed meat rolls)

Thinly sliced veal, 11 ounces
Lean meat of milk fed veal, 2½ ounces
Lean ham, 1½ ounces
Marrow of veal, one ounce
Grated Parmesan, one ounce
One egg

It is customary to cut about six or seven pieces from the meat, three inches square; flatten the slices with the handle of a knife, dipping the handle into cold water to extend the meat well. Chop the ham together finely with the 2½ ounces of lean milk-fed veal. Beat the marrow with the blade of knife till it is reduced to a paste; add Parmesan and mix all with the egg. Add a pinch of pepper. Now stretch the veal slices (braciuoline) and in the middle of each place an even share of this stuffing. Roll them, and tie them crosswise with string.

Now make a fricassee by chopping together a small onion, a piece of celery, a piece of carrot, less than one ounce of dry meat of some kind and place it on the fire in a pan with ⅔ ounce of butter, together with the meat rolls. Add a pinch of salt and pepper. When the fricassee is browned, pour in tomato sauce and allow it to cook slowly, adding as much water as necessary till the meat is well done. A few drops of white wine would not be out of place. Remove the string and serve.

190 — ROLLS OF LOIN OF PORK
(Braciuoline nella scamerita)

This is a typically Florentine dish. Place the pork chops in a pot with very little oil, two or three cloves of garlic together with the skin, and some salt and pepper sprinkled on the meat. When browned on both sides, pour in about ⅓ glass of red wine and allow it to boil till half of the gravy has been absorbed. Now remove the meat and keep it warm. Take a boiled black cabbage, squeeze the water from it, cut it finely, and place it in the gravy. Add some salt and pepper and allow it to cook for a while. Serve the rolls on top of the cabbage.

191 — BRACIUOLINE IN PEASANT STYLE

Prepare the rolls with lean veal which has been flattened well; smear them with oil, and season them with a little salt and pepper. Make a mixture of pickled olives, capers and an anchovy, and chop everything finely. Add the yolk of an egg and a pinch of Parmesan cheese, if desired. Stuff the braciuoline, tie them, and cook them in butter and tomato sauce, or in an onion fricassee.

192 — HAM CUTLETS

Cut some veal meat into thin slices, flatten them with a large knife blade, and cut the slices into pieces, 3 inches square. Dip each piece into beaten egg together with a slice of ham half the size of the cutlet. Holding both the cutlet and the ham together dip them into grated bread; sprinkle with salt, and brown them together in butter, the side with the ham downward. Remove, and place thin slices of either Parmesan or Gruyere cheese on top of the ham. Now replace them in pot, and finish cooking by placing the pot under the fire in the oven. Serve these cutlets with meat gravy and lemon juice. If preferred, tomato gravy serves the purpose as well.

193 — MEAT BALLS

I do not pretend to describe a novel dish here. The art of making meat balls is quite well known, but a suggestion here and there will not do harm. I am referring to meat balls made with boiled meat, but if raw meat is preferred, less ingredients for seasoning should be used.

Chop the boiled meat in a mortar. Chop a slice of ham separately. Add the ham to the meat and season everything with Parmesan, salt, pepper, and some flavor of spice. Add some raisins, pine seeds and two spoonfuls of bread, boiled either in soup or milk. Bind this compound with an egg or two, according to the quantity. Make meat balls as large as an egg, flatten them at both ends, cover them with grated bread and fry them in oil or lard. Make a fricassee with a little garlic and parsley, place it in a flat pan together with the fat left in the pan where the meat balls were fried, and add the meat balls. Sprinkle on egg-lemon sauce and let it take on flavor. If the garlic-parsley fricassee is objectionable, place the meat balls in the flat pan with a piece of butter only.

194 — POLPETTONE (*Meat Loaf*)

This meat loaf is made with pick-ups of boiled meat, and in spite of its simplicity, it is quite palatable. Remove the fat from the meat and chop the lean part of it in a mortar. Add sufficient salt, pepper, Parmesan cheese, an egg or two, and two spoonfuls of boiled bread. Mix all these ingredients and form the meat loaf into an oval shape. Cover it with flour. Fry it in lard or oil so as to form a crust on the outside. Remove it from the pan and place it in a pot with a piece of butter and let it fry on both sides. When the meat loaf is done and about to be served, beat two eggs in a separate dish, or pan, add a pinch of salt and the juice of half a lemon, as if it were a cream sauce, and pour it on the meat loaf. When turning the meat loaf in the pan, do not use a spoon or fork, but follow the rules for turning an omelet; use a dish, so as not to break the loaf before serving it.

195 — MEAT LOAF MADE WITH RAW MEAT IN FLORENTINE STYLE

Remove all visible film from a little more than a pound of boneless veal meat and chop it, first with a knife, then with a meat chopper, together with a slice of ham. Add salt and pepper, some spice and an egg. Mix well with your hand, form the meat into a ball and cover it with flour.

Now, chop a small onion together with a little carrot, celery and parsley and place it on the fire in a pot with oil, adding a small piece of butter. When it has browned, place the meat loaf on top of it. Allow it to brown on all sides and then pour in half a glass of water mixed with a spoonful of flour. Cover it well and let it cook on a low fire without sticking to the pot. When about to be served in its own gravy, squeeze half a lemon on it.

If you wish to make this meat loaf in the Piemontese style, place a hard boiled egg in the middle of the loaf when forming it. In cutting the loaf into slices, the egg would then look rather fancy. This is a palatable dish.

Cut two cloves of garlic into thin slices and stick them into ¾ lbs. of leg of lamb together with a little bunch of rosemary leaves. It must be a bunch without loose leaves, so as to be removed easily from the meat. Chop finely together some dry meat and a piece of lardon, and place it in a pot with the lamb and a little oil. Add salt and pepper, and allow it to brown. Add a piece of butter, some tomato sauce, or some diluted tomato paste and allow it to cook slowly. Remove the lamb from the pot for a while and place the peas in the gravy. Let them boil a short time and then place the lamb on top of them. Allow the peas and the lamb to cook together and serve the peas as a side dish.

In this same style, one can prepare a piece of veal from the rump or the flank. In Tuscany these dishes are cooked in the same manner, but a little oil is added.

197 — LAMB FRICASSEE (*Trippato*)

Cut a pound of lamb from the flank into pieces. Fry it in virgin lard. Then, with fat from the fried lamb, make a sauce with some garlic and parsley in a separate pot. When the garlic has browned, add the already fried lamb. Add salt and pepper, stir it well and often and allow it to remain on the fire till it has taken on flavor.

Now prepare the following sauce: Beat two eggs and a goodly pinch of Parmesan cheese with half a lemon. Pour it on the lamb, mix well, and as soon as the egg is condensed, serve.

198 — SHOULDER OF LAMB IN HUNGARIAN STYLE

Indeed the name matters little. You may call it anything you wish as long as the dish succeeds and is palatable.

Cut the shoulder of lamb into good-sized pieces. Chop either two onions or four white scallions and fry them with a piece of butter. As soon as the onion browns, add the lamb, salt and pepper. When the meat browns, cover it with flour and add another piece of butter. Mix well and let it cook slowly in soup added gradually, a little at a time. Serve with a good deal of gravy.

199 — HEAD OF LAMB

To make a stew with the head of a lamb, do not follow the example of the maid who was told to cut the head into two parts, and cut it crosswise. The head must be cut lengthwise. Now prepare a little fricassee with garlic, parsley and oil. As soon as the garlic browns, add a ladleful of stock soup. Place the head in it, add salt and pepper, and allow it to boil. When half done, add a piece of butter, a little tomato sauce, and let it cook till it is done. Add more stock soup, if necessary.

This is not a dish for guests, but it is an inexpensive one for the family. The part around the eye is the most palatable.

200 — STEW OF MUSCLES

It is well known that the muscles of an animal are the bundles of fibre which constitute meat in general. But muscles for the Florentines is that part of the veal which lies between the extreme end of the haunch or the shoulder and extends toward the legs, and contains tender and gelatinous tendons quite palatable when cooked in the following way.

Cut a little over one pound of veal muscle into pieces. Place it on the fire in a little oil and two cloves of crushed garlic, peel and all. Allow it to fry a while and add the meat. Add enough salt and pepper. When browned, sprinkle a spoonful of flour on it, add some tomato sauce or diluted tomato paste and a piece of butter. Add sufficient stock soup or water, little by little, till the meat is well done. Be sure that there is some gravy left in the pot, after the meat is cooked. Arrange slices of toasted bread in a dish, pour the stew on them and serve. The stew may be served without toast, by adding sliced fresh mushrooms when the meat is about done.

201 — STEW OF BREAST OF MILK-FED VEAL WITH FENNEL

Cut the breast of milk-fed veal, bone and all, into pieces. Chop together some garlic, parsley, celery and carrot. Place this on the fire with oil, pepper and salt, and add the meat. Turn the meat over often and when browned, sprinkle a pinch of flour, a little tomato sauce or diluted tomato paste on it, and allow it to cook by adding gradually some stock soup or water. When about half done, add a piece of butter and the roughly cut fennel, which is to be half cooked in boiling water and fried in butter beforehand. Remember that in cooking stews, the pot must be tightly covered throughout.

202 — MILK-FED VEAL IN GUAZZETTO
(*In Special Gravy*)

This gravy will not be a delicacy, but it is a simple, nourishing food. Use that part of the veal called the rump.

For about 17 ounces of boneless meat, place 1 ounce of butter and 1 ounce of sliced dry meat in a layer in the pot. On top of this layer place half a lemon, cut into four slices, rind and seeds removed. Now place the veal on top of this. Flatten and tie the meat neatly and place it in the pot above the other ingredients. Allow it to brown, but be careful it doesn't stick on account of the small quantity of gravy used. When browned, drain the superfluous fat, add some salt and pepper and pour in a glass of boiled, warm milk. It does not matter if the milk coagulates. Cover the pot with a double sheet of paper and allow the meat to cook on a low fire till it is done. When about to serve, pass the gravy through a cloth or fine sieve.

This amount is usually sufficient for four diners.

203 — STUFFED BREAST OF MILK-FED VEAL

Breast of milk-fed veal, one piece, 1 pound ,
Lean milk-fed veal, boneless, 6 ounces
Fat and lean ham, 1 ounce
Bologna, 1 ounce
Grated Parmesan, ½ ounce
Egg, 1
A fourth of a clove of garlic
Parsley

Clean the lean veal and chop it finely with a bit of fat ham. Add the finely chopped garlic and parsley, the Parmesan, the egg, season with salt and pepper, and mix everything.

Remove the hard bones from the breast of veal; cut it open passing a knife under the ribs. On the part of the breast with the bones spread part of the mixture and on top of this place part of the ham and Bologna which has been cut into strips. Add a second and a third layer, following the same sequence. Now cover the stuffing with the other part of the breast of veal and sew up the edges so that the stuffing cannot escape. Tie the meat crosswise and lengthwise. Put in on the fire in a casserole with a piece of butter, salt and pepper, and when it is browned on both sides, cook it by adding water a little at a time.

Serve hot. Remove the string and cut it into slices. A side dish of peas cooked in the meat sauce, or of stewed fennel can be used.

204 — BEEF SEASONED WITH CLOVES

One can have a choice as to the quality of the meat. It may be beef or veal, according to preference.

Flatten a goodly piece of meat from the leg or the rump well, and place it in wine the evening before. If the piece weighs about 2¼ lbs., stick a few slices of lardon and four cloves into it; tie it well and place it on the fire in a pot with half a sliced onion, abundant oil and butter in equal amounts, and some salt. Brown it on all sides. When the onion is well done, pour in a glassful of water. Place a double sheet of paper on the pot and then cover it and let the contents boil slowly, till done. Untie the string from the meat, pass the gravy through a cloth, separate the pieces of lardon and sprinkle some salt and pepper on them. Serve the meat with its own gravy. This is a dish for healthy stomachs.

205 — TRIPE WITH SAUCE

Tripe is an ordinary dish in whatever style it is cooked. Delicate stomachs do not favor it, but they are more likely to do so if it is cooked in Milanese style, for the Milanese have learned to prepare it so as to make it light and tender. You may be able to buy the tripe already boiled, in which case it saves work. If it is raw, boil the tripe yourself. In buying it, choose the one that is girded with a rope-like edge. After boiling it cut it into ribbon-like strips, ½ inch wide, and dry them in a canvas towel. Place them in a pot and fry them with butter. When the tripe has absorbed the butter, add some meat gravy or tomato sauce. Add salt and pepper and let it cook till well done. When about to remove it from the fire, sprinkle a pinch of Parmesan cheese over it.

206 — TRIPE WITH EGGS

Boil and cut the tripe as described in the preceding recipe. Place it on the fire in a fricassee of garlic, parsley and butter. Add salt and pepper, and when done, bind it with two beaten eggs, some lemon juice and Parmesan cheese.

207 — TRIPE IN CORSICAN STYLE

This is a most palatable tripe dish, and is also quite easily digested. However, the secret of its specialty lies in the fact that it is necessary to cook it in abundant meat gravy. Furthermore, this kind of meat gravy for tripe can be prepared only by using the feet of bovine beasts cleaned of their bristles, because that callous cuticle is very good for the gravy.

Raw tripe, less than 2 lbs.
Boneless feet, 3½ ounces
Butter, 2½ ounces
Lard, 2 ounces
Half a large onion
Two small cloves of garlic
Flavor of nutmeg and spices
Sufficient meat gravy
A goodly pinch of Parmesan

After having washed the tripe thoroughly, cut it into ribbon-like strips ½ inch wide. Do likewise with the feet. Dice the onion and place it in a pot on the fire with butter. When it has taken on color, add the lardon minced together with garlic. When this fricassee has browned lightly, add the tripe and the feet; add salt, pepper and the rest of the spices, but be sure not to indulge in too much spice. Allow the tripe to boil till dry and then add the meat gravy. Let it boil slowly till the tripe has become tender. This ordinarily would take from 7 to 8 hours. In case the meat gravy runs short, add some stock soup. When about to serve, flavor it with Parmesan and spread it on toast with abundant gravy.

This quantity is usually sufficient for five servings.

208 — MILK-FED VEAL LIVER IN
MILITARY STYLE

Chop a scallion or a new onion finely; allow it to fry in oil and butter. When it has become dark brown, add the liver, cut into thin slices. When the liver is half done, add salt, pepper and a pinch of chopped parsley. Allow it to boil slowly till done. Serve it in its own gravy, but squeeze the juice of half a lemon into the gravy. In this case, and other similar cases, to remove the sourness from the scallion or onion, place it in a canvas towel immersed in fresh water; then squeeze the water out thoroughly before cooking it.

209 — MUTTON LOIN CUTLETS AND VEAL CHOPS IN FINANZIERE STYLE

Place a slice of ham, some butter and a little bunch of aromatic herbs, composed of carrot, celery, and sprigs of parsley, in a pot. Lay the mutton cutlets on top whole. Add salt and pepper. Let the cutlets brown on both sides; add another piece of butter if necessary, and place some chicken liver, sweetbreads and sliced fresh mushrooms between the cutlets. When all these ingredients are browned, add sufficient stock soup and allow the cutlets to cook over a low fire. Bind the gravy with a pinch of flour. Boil half a glass of white wine till it is reduced to one-half, and add it to the cutlets. When done, allow them to boil a little longer so as to allow the meat to absorb the flavor. When about to serve, remove the ham and the bunch of aromatic herbs; strain the gravy and remove the fat from it.

Veal chops can be prepared in the same style, adding some peas to the above ingredients. This is a very delicious dish if prepared carefully.

210 — FILETTO WITH MARSALA WINE
(Sirloin)

Filetto (Sirloin) is the most tender of meats, but do not get a piece full of tendons, for this would spoil the dish.

If 2¼ lbs. of sirloin are to be prepared, roll it and tie it neatly. Place it on the fire, adding a sliced onion, a few thin slices of ham and a piece of butter. Add salt and pepper. When browned on all sides, and when the onion is well done, sprinkle a pinch of flour on it. Let it take on color and add enough stock soup or water. Allow it to boil slowly, then pass the gravy through a cloth or soup strainer, remove the fat from it, add half a glass of marsala wine, and replace the gravy in the pot together with the meat. Boil slowly till meat is done and gravy is condensed. Do not put too much flour in the gravy. Serve filetto with its own gravy.

211 — MEAT IN GENOESE STYLE

Thoroughly flatten a lean steak of veal of about 1 pound. Beat three or four eggs, add sufficient salt and pepper, a pinch of Parmesan cheese, some chopped parsley, and fry the eggs in butter as an omelet, the size of the piece of meat. Stretch this omelet on the meat so as to cover it entirely. Trim the omelet wherever necessary and add the small pieces to cover the uncovered parts of the meat. This done, roll the veal and the omelet together, tie it neatly, sprinkle flour on it and place it in a pot with butter. Add salt and pepper. When browned on all sides, add sufficient stock soup and allow it to cook slowly. Serve it with its own gravy which, due to the flour, will be somewhat dense.

212 — PIE OF SEMOLINO AND
MEAT STUFFING

Pies with meat stuffings are generally a compound of slices of meat, chicken liver, etc. and vegetables, rice or semolino. If you choose semolino, see recipe No. 141. Mix the butter and the Parmesan cheese with the entire mixture of ingredients and place it in a pie dish or form which has been buttered and whose bottom has been covered with a sheet of paper. The meat stuffing to be placed in the semolino or in the center hole of the form must be cooked in gravy with truffles or fresh mushrooms. Cook this pie in a double boiler and serve it hot with gravy spread on top.

213 — PIE OF RICE WITH GRAVY AND CHICKEN LIVER

Prepare a savory meat gravy to be used both for the rice and the chicken liver. To the latter add a slice of ham fried in butter, seasoned with salt and pepper, and cook it separately in the meat gravy. The flavor of truffles or mushrooms adds taste to the dish.

Allow the rice to fry in butter, dry it, then finish cooking it in boiling water. Add some meat gravy and a pinch of Parmesan. Beat two eggs to eleven ounces of rice, and add them when the rice is done and has somewhat cooled off.

Spread butter on the surface of a smooth round or oval pot, cover the bottom with paper smeared with butter and place the rice on it. Bake the rice in the oven. On removing the rice from the form, pour the chicken liver gravy, condensed by a pinch of flour, on it. Serve it with the chicken liver and with abundant gravy.

214 — GENOESE PUDDING *(Budino)*

Milk-fed veal, 5 ounces
One chicken breast, 4 ounces
Ham, less than 2 ounces
Butter, 1 ounce
Grated Parmesan, ⅔ ounce
Eggs, 3
Flavor of nutmeg
Pinch of salt

Chop finely the veal, chicken breast and ham in a mortar, together with the butter, the Parmesan and a piece of crustless bread soaked in milk. Chop everything fine enough to pass through a sieve. Add 3 spoonfuls of a delicate and savory sauce of your choice, and mix well.

Smear a smooth form of white metal with butter and at the bottom place a sheet of paper cut to size and also smeared with butter. Pour the compound on it and place it in another pan with boiling water; cook it as in a double boiler arrangement. When you remove the pudding from the form and place it in a dish, add some chicken liver, cooked in meat gravy. Serve while hot.

215 — MACARONI PUDDING

The cooks of Romagna are experts in preparing this costly and rather complicated dish. It is an excellent course if carefully prepared, and is popular in Romagna during carnival time.

The best style of macaroni for this pie is the long Neapolitan type with a hole length-wise, because it absorbs abundant gravy. Here are the ingredients sufficient for 12 people.

Macaroni, 12 ounces
Parmesan, 6 ounces
Sweet-breads, 5 ounces
Butter, 2 ounces
Truffles, 2½ ounces
Ham, 1 ounce
A handful of dry mushrooms
Liver and kidneys of 3 or 4 chickens, together with their crests and eggs
Flavor of nutmeg

Do not be frightened by this large quantity of ingredients, for they will disappear under the crust of the dough.

Boil the macaroni in salt water until they are half done; remove them dry and place them in gravy No. 4. Allow them to absorb the gravy cooking slowly on a low fire.

In the meantime prepare the following sauce: Place a spoonful of flour with a piece of butter as large as an egg on the fire. Mix the flour well in the melting butter, and when light brown, pour in a pint of milk, a little at a time. Stir steadily till it is condensed into a milky cream-like liquid. If this sauce is too thick, thin it by replacing it on the fire with another piece of butter mixed with flour.

Cook the chicken livers in butter, adding sufficient gravy gradually. Season with salt and pepper. Cut the sweet-breads into pieces of one inch and cook; add the ham sliced thinly together with the truffles, also sliced in the same way. Soak the dry mushrooms in warm water, add flavor of nutmeg and mix all these ingredients together.

By this time you should have ready the crust dough, as directed in recipe No. 341A, with the flavor of lemon rind added. Fill the pie as follows: Smear as large a dish as you need with butter; remove the superfluous gravy from the macaroni and place the first layer in your dish, seasoning it with grated Parmesan cheese, a piece of butter here and there, a spoonful of white sauce and the other ingredients. Repeat the operation till you have filled the dish. Roll the crust dough to the thickness of a silver dollar coin, first with a smooth rolling pin, then with a grooved one, and cover the stuffing down to the bottom with the dough. Cut dough strips 1½ inches wide and as long as necessary, and place them cross-wise on top. Place a strip, as wide as the depth of the dish, around the stuffing, and if you have a taste for fancy decoration, do your best at it with the remainder of the dough. Gild the entire surface with beaten egg and place it in the oven to bake. Serve this dish while hot.

216 — PIE OF FRICASSEE

Make a sauce with the following:

Flour, 5 ounces
Butter, 2 ounces
Parmesan cheese, 1 ounce
Eggs, 3
More than 1 pint of milk
A small bunch of spinach; sufficient salt

Boil the spinach and pass it through a sieve. Break the eggs into the sauce when about to withdraw it from the fire. Add the spinach to only half of the sauce.

Smear with cold butter either a copper dish or a form with a hole in the middle and grooved all around. Pour the green sauce in first, then the yellow. Place it in a double boiler and allow it to condense. Remove the sauce from the form while warm and place in the middle hole either a fricassee of chicken liver or thin slices of milk-fed veal seasoned with truffles or mushrooms. Finish cooking this *manicaretto* either with butter or with meat gravy, taking care that it takes on a savory taste. This dish will surely draw forth praise from the guests.

217 — PIE OF RICE AND CHICKEN LIVER

Rice, 5 ounces
Parmesan cheese, 1 ounce
Butter, ¾ ounce
Over 1 pint of milk
Eggs, 3
Sufficient salt

Cook the rice in milk and add butter. Salt it and when cold add the rest of the ingredients. Place it in a circular form with a hole in the middle and with a buttered sheet of paper at the bottom. Place this in a double boiler and let it cook for a short time so that it does not thicken too much. Remove while warm and place chicken liver in the middle hole.

This quantity is usually enough for five.

218 — PIGEON ROAST WITH PEAS

The best way to prepare pigeons is to roast them with peas. Roast them on top of some chopped onion, ham, oil and butter. As they take on color, add either water or stock soup and allow them to cook slowly. Pass the gravy through a cloth, remove the fat, and cook the peas in it. Place peas around pigeons when serving.

219 — POT ROAST OF BOILED MEAT

If you wish to give a savory taste to boiled meat, prepare it as follows: If 2½ pounds of meat is used, remove it from the soup before it is well done. Place it in a roaster on top of a fricassee of dry meat, onion, celery, carrot and a piece of butter. Season with salt, pepper and spices. When the fricassee in well done, add some tomato sauce and allow the meat to cook. Strain the gravy and remove the fat from it. Then replace it on the fire with the meat and a handful of soaked dry mushrooms.

220 — OSSO-BUCO

This is a Milanese specialty, but I will describe it for you as well as I can. Osso-buco is a piece of bone with meat around it and a hole in the center. It is either the leg or the shoulder of milk-fed veal. It is usually cooked in a sort of pot roast style.

Prepare as many pieces as there are guests. Place the meat on top of chopped onion, celery, carrot and a piece of butter. Add salt and pepper. When browned, add another piece of butter mixed with flour so as to color it and bind the gravy. Add some water, some tomato sauce, and allow it to cook slowly. Strain the gravy and remove the fat. Replace it on the fire with the meat and season it with chopped lemon rind. When about to remove from the fire, add a pinch of chopped parsley.

221 — TONGUE ALLA SCARLATTA
(Scarlet Style)

It is called scarlet style because the tongue takes on a scarlet color. If prepared carefully it will be a palatable dish. Take either a tongue of veal or one of beef and rub it with about one ounce of saltpetre till it has been absorbed by the tongue. After 24 hours, wash the tongue as many times as necessary in cold water to remove the saltpetre, and while still wet, rub it with a good deal of salt. Leave the tongue in the salt for 8 days, turning it over every morning.

The best way to cook the tongue is to boil it. Set it on the fire in cold water, using some of the salt water in which it has been cured, a little bunch of aromatic herbs and half an onion with some cloves stuck in it. Allow it to boil 3 or 4 hours. Remove the skin while the tongue it still hot; let it cool off and serve. To improve the dish add a side dish of jelly No. 3. The tongue can be served as a warm dish by adding potato or spinach at the side. This is a dish to be preferred for Winter months.

222 — VEAL WITH SAUCE OF TUNA FISH

(Vitello Tonnato)

Remove all the cuticles or fat from a piece of 2½ pounds of leg or rump of milk-fed veal. Stick the clean and boneless filet of two anchovies cut into 8 pieces into it. Tie the meat rather loosely Place enough cold water to cover the meat in a pot, together with ¼ of an onion stuck with 2 cloves, a laurel leaf, celery, carrot and parsley. Salt the water generously, and when boiling place the meat in it. Allow the meat to boil about an hour and a half. Untie the meat, dry it well and season it by placing it for 3 days in a small vase together with the following sauce: Chop 3 ounces of tuna fish preserved in olive oil together with two anchovies. Mash it well or pass it through a fine sieve. Add, a little at a time, abundant fine olive oil and the juice of a whole lemon so as to make a liquid sauce. Then squeeze the vinegar from a goodly quantity of pickled capers and add them. Serve the cold veal thinly sliced with the sauce and lemon slices. The soup may be strained and used for cooking a dish of rice.

223 — CAPON IN GALANTINE

In describing this capon, I have in mind one which I once cooked in my own home for ten guests. When all the feathers and bones were discarded from the capon, and it was stuffed with the necessary ingredients, it sufficed for twenty guests. After the insides were cleaned and the bones removed as directed in No. 163 it was stuffed with the following ingredients:

Lean meat of milk-fed veal, 7 ounces
Lean pork meat, 7 ounces
Half a breast of chicken
Salt pork, 4 ounces
Ham, lean and fat mixed, 1½ ounces
Black truffles, 1½ ounces
Pistachio nuts, ⅔ ounces
Salted tongue, 3 ounces

If pork is not available, breast of turkey is a good substitute. Cut the truffles into pieces as large as a nut. Remove the shells of the pistachio in warm water and slice the rest of the ingredients into thin slices about ½ inch wide. Put these aside for the time being while salting the meats.

Take another 7 ounces of miik-fed veal and lean pork and chop it together, apart from the above ingredients. Mash this in a mortar together with 2 ounces of bread crumbs soaked in stock soup. Add an egg, the skin of the truffles, the scraps of the tongue and ham, season it all with salt and when all is well mashed, pass it through a fine sieve.

Now, spread open the capon, sprinkle some salt on it, and begin to place the stuffing in the following manner: First a layer of the mashed mixture, then a layer of the slices of the meats with here and there a piece of truffle and pistachio. Repeat the operation till you have used up all the ingredients, but place the slices of breast of chicken towards the lower end of the capon so as not to place the same quality of meat together. Now pull together the two sides of the capon and sew it up as well as you can. Tie it lengthwise with a string, wrap it tightly with a cloth, tie the two ends of the cloth and boil it in water for two and a half hours. Untie the cloth and wash it, then rewrap the capon in the same cloth, and place it on a flat surface. Place a weight on the breast of the capon and leave it in that position for two hours so that it flattens considerably.

The water in which the capon was boiled is good for stock soup or for jelly No. 3.

224 — ARISTA, PORK LOIN IN CHOPS

That part of the loin of pork which is cut together with the bone from the back of the animal is called Arista in Tuscany. The Tuscans eat it cold because they consider it tastier. The entire piece should weigh about ten pounds.

Make small openings in the meat and insert some garlic, pieces of rosemary leaves and some clove, all in small portions, because these aromas are apt to repeat. Season the meat with salt and pepper. Cook it either on the griddle or in the oven. The fat which trickles from the meat can be used to cook vegetables or bake potatoes. This is a family dish in Winter time because it can be kept for a few days.

225 — COLD PARTRIDGE PIE

It is possible to make a partridge pie for six or seven people out of one gray or black partridge. These belong to the species of Rasores. They feed on vegetables, especially grains, and therefore develop a belly and fat sides. They are found on mountains in temperate countries. Their meat is excellent, but of the two birds, the black partridge is to be preferred.

Tender Partridge, 1
Chicken livers, 3
Egg yolk, 1
Laurel leaves, 2
Marsala wine, ⅓ of a glass
Black truffles, 2 ounces (or a little less)
Salted tongue, 2 ounces (or a little less)
Ham, both lean and fat, 1 ounce
Butter, 1 ounce
Bread crumbs, 1 cup
A little onion, carrot, celery, chopped together
Some soup stock

Clean the partridge, wash it and place it on the fire with the chopped onion, carrot and celery, together with butter, ham (sliced thinly) and two bay leaves. Season it with salt and pepper. When the onion is brown, add, little by little, the Marsala wine, and if this is not enough, add some stock soup till be partridge is half done. Remove the partridge from the fire and cut off the entire breast from the bird. Cut this into eight slices and set them aside. Cut the rest, including the liver of the partridge, into small pieces and cook it together with the chicken liver.

When these ingredients are cooked, remove them dry from the pan. Remove the bay leaves and place everything in a mortar. Soak the bread crumbs in the remaining gravy; add some stock soup and mix it well. Add this, together with scrappings of the truffles, to the ingredients in the mortar. Mash all very well and pass it through a fine sieve. Add the egg yolk and work the entire mixture till it has become paste-like.

— 149 —

Now prepare the crust dough as directed in recipe No. 229.

For the pie use one of those special pans with hinged cover, made of white metal and round or oval in shape. Smear this pan with butter and cover its bottom with crust dough of the thickness of a silver dollar. Place this in a regular pie dish, also smeared with butter.

Make a layer with part of the mixture, then add part of the slices of breast of partridge and tongue, alternating with pieces of raw truffles till all the ingredients are used up. Now flatten it so as to make it a compact mass, and cover it with the crust dough, adding some little decoration on top. Make a hole in the center for the escape of vapor. Gild the top of the pie and cook it in the oven.

When removing the pie from the oven, cover the center hole with a tassel made with the same crust dough, which has been cooked separately.

226 — RABBIT BREAD

Here in another recipe for a cold dish.

Lean rabbit meat, 9 ounces
Butter, 3½ oz.
Flour, 1¾ ounces
Grated cheese (Parmesan), 1 ounce
Egg yolks, 6
Milk, 1 pint

Chop finely ⅔ oz. of ham with a little onion. Place it on the fire with half of the butter and the rabbit meat cut into small pieces. Season with salt.

When the fat has been absorbed and before the meat browns up, add stock soup and let it cook. When done, mash the meat in the mortar, moistening it with its own gravy (as you work it), and pass it through a sieve.

Make a sauce with the flour, the remainder of the butter and the milk. Wait until it is cool and beat the egg yolks into it. Mix everything together. Smear a sheet of paper with butter, cover the bottom of a smooth form with it and cook the meat in a double boiler.

Serve it cold, surrounded by jelly. It would be a grateful surprise to diners if the rabbit bread would be brought to the table entirely covered with jelly. This can be done by simply covering the bottom of a larger dish than that which has been used for the rabbit bread with jelly. Place the meat on it and fill the empty space with liquid jelly. Wait till the jelly has cooled off and serve it as a surprise.

227 — LIVER BREAD

Of all the cold dishes I am describing the following is one of the most savory ones.

Liver of milk-fed veal, 18 ounces
Butter, 2½ ounces
Fresh crustless bread, 2 ounces
Grated Parmesan, ¾ ounce
Chicken livers, 4
Marsala wine, 1 wine glass
Meat soup, 6 tablesp.
Eggs, 3 (1 whole; 2 yolks)
Bay leaf, 1
Sufficient salt and pepper

Cut the liver into thin slices. Cut each chicken liver into two parts. Place all in a frying pan with ½ of the butter and the bay leaf. As soon as the butter has been absorbed, throw in the other half and season the liver with salt and pepper. Pour in the Marsala wine, and after 4 or 5 minutes of strong frying, when the liver is still tender, remove it and mash it in a mortar. Now shred the bread into the gravy left in the pan, mix it, and throw it, too, into the mortar, then pass everything through a sieve. Add the Parmesan and the eggs, diluting the compound with the soup. Place this compound in a double boiler and let it harden. When lukewarm, remove it. When cooled off, place it in a larger dish and cover it with jelly No. 3.

This quantity is sufficient for 12.

228 — LIVER PIE

Make use of the compound described above, adding 1 ounce of sliced black truffles, heated to the boiling point in marsala wine, before mixing. Cover it with pie crust No. 229 and baked it in a country oven. Serve cold.

229 — RABBIT MEAT PIE

Those who are not disposed to work hard should not try to prepare this dish. The nature of the meat and the bony structure of the animal require much work.

The description that follows is that of an actual preparation made in my presence.

Half a rabbit, without head or legs, 2⅓ lbs.
Lean milk-fed veal, 9 ounces
Butter, 3½ ounces
Salted tongue, 2½ ounces
Fat of ham, 2½ ounces
Ham, lean and fat, sliced ¼ inch thick, less than 2 ounces
Black truffles, 2 ounces
Flour for sauce, 1 ounce
Marsala wine, ½ pt. (good measure)
Eggs, 2
Milk, ½ glass
Sufficient soup stock

Wash the rabbit and dry it. Remove about 3 ounces of lean meat from the loins, or any other part of it, and set this aside. Then remove all the flesh from the bones and set these aside also. Cut the meat into pieces, and together with the 3 ounces of lean meat left in a single piece pickle it in ⅔ of the marsala wine, with a quarter of a large onion, half a carrot, the whole length of a sprig of celery, several sprigs of parsley and two bay leaves. Add salt and pepper; turn it over often, and allow it to remain in this solution for several hours. In the meantime, remove all visible film from the veal and cut it first with a knife and then chop it finely in a mortar.

Drain the marsala wine from the meat and place it on the fire in a pan together with the bones, the aromatic herbs, the fat of ham cut into small pieces, and 1 ounce of butter. Cover it and allow it to brown over a strong fire. Turn it often, and when dry, moisten it with marsala wine, also using that which was drained from the meat. Add soup stock till the meat is well done. Now separate the meat again from the bones and set the single piece aside (3 ounces). This piece, the 2 ounces of ham and the tongue should be cut into slices about 2 inches thick.

First chop the rabbit meat in the mortar, moistening it at intervals, in order to make it liquid, with the remainder of the marsala wine and some soup stock. Pass it through a fine sieve. Break and chop the bones as finely as possible and pass the fine part of them through a metal sieve. Now make a sauce with 1 ounce of the above butter, the flour and the milk. When this is cooked, add the meat passed through a sieve (rabbit and raw milk-fed veal). Add eggs, mix well and taste the mixture to assure yourself of the seasoning. If necessary, add salt and the rest of the butter.

Now form the pie with crust dough, as described in recipe No. 225. Cut truffles into pieces the size of a nut, mix them with the slices of meat mentioned above, and without cooking them, place them in layers alternating with the mixture. Flatten the compound well and see that the layers are well arranged so as to show a nice pattern when the pie is cut into slices. Finally, place the thin slices of ham on it, and cover it with crust made of the following:

Flour, 9 ounces
Butter, 3 ounces
Wine alcohol, 2 teaspoons
Sugar, 2 teaspoons
Egg yolks, 2
Lemon, 1 slice
A pinch of salt
Cold water, if necessary

Following this recipe, meat pies with several kinds

of venison, as wild boar, deer and roe-buck, can be made.

230 — STUFFED YOUNG SQUASH

Before stuffing the squash cut it in half, either lengthwise or crosswise. If you prefer, you may leave it whole. Remove the seeds with a tin tube. Be sure to carve a large enough space so that enough stuffing can be placed in it.

Now prepare the stuffing with lean milk-fed veal. Cut the meat into pieces and place it in a pan with a fricassee of onion, parsley, celery, carrot, a few small pieces of dry meat, oil, salt and pepper. Turn it over often. When the meat has absorbed the oil and taken on color, add a ladleful of water. When this water has been absorbed add another ladleful, and, a little later another, so as to allow the meat to cook and to leave some gravy. Remove the gravy, pass it through a cloth and set it apart.

Chop the meat finely, add an egg, some grated Parmesan, bread crumbs boiled either in stock soup or milk, and some spices. Mix well into a compound and use this as stuffing. Now fry the stuffed squash in butter till it is light brown, then add the gravy you set aside previously and allow it to cook.

231 — YOUNG SQUASH WITH FISH STUFFING

Prepare the squash as in the preceding recipe and stuff it with a compound made of chopped tuna fish preserved in oil, mixed with an egg. a pinch of Parmesan, a little of the core of the same squash, some spices and a little pepper. Fry it in butter, and when it has taken on a light brown color, season with tomato sauce No. 78. If prepared with care, this dish will be satisfactory.

232 — STRING BEANS AND YOUNG SQUASH SAUTE'

These are side-dish vegetables. Fine cooking favors simple seasoning. This is certainly beneficial for the digestive process, but it is doubtful that taste gains by it. If you are preparing string beans, boil them till they are half done. If it is young squash, cut it into thin slices or short pieces without boiling it. When so prepared, fry it in butter. When the butter has browned lightly, add salt and pepper. To add flavor to the dish, add some tomato sauce No. 78.

233 — STRING BEANS WITH EGG SAUCE

Remove the string from ¾ lbs. of string beans and boil them in salted water till they are half done. Remove them from the water, dry them, cut them into small pieces of about one inch, cook them in butter and season them with salt and pepper. Beat an egg yolk together with a spoonful of flour and the juice of ¼ of a lemon. Dilute it with a ladleful of cold lean soup and place the liquid on the fire in a small pan. Mix well and stir steadily till it has boiled to the consistency of flowing cream. Pour it on the string beans, keeping them on the fire till the sauce has been absorbed. Serve the string beans as a side dish to boiled meats. To retain the fresh green color of these vegetables, add bicarbonate of soda while boiling.

234 — STRING BEANS WITH WHITE SAUCE
(*Balsamella*)

While boiling the string beans, add a teaspoonful of soda so they retain their fresh greenness. Fry them in butter for a short time and season them with salt and pepper. Add some thin white sauce made with cream, butter and flour, and serve them dressed with fried bread, cut into small ovals. It is a fine side-dish.

235 — STRING BEANS WITH VANILLA FLAVOR

Soak the string beans in fresh water, and if they are tender, cook them as follows:

Make a fricassee with oil, a scallion, a young onion, parsley, carrot and celery. Season it with salt and pepper and when browned, add some soup and pass it through a cloth. Add some tomato sauce to this gravy and then pour in the string beans. While they boil, flavor with two spoonfuls of sugar and a dash of vanilla.

236 — STRING BEANS, ARETINA STYLE

Remove both ends (tips) and cut each bean into three parts. Place the string beans in a pan with two cloves of garlic, fresh tomato sauce and cold water to cover them. Season with oil, salt and pepper, and allow them to boil slowly till done. Do not allow them to become dry. This dish can be served as a side dish with boiled meat.

237 — BEANS ALL'UCCELLETTO

In the restaurants of Florence loose fresh beans are said to be all'uccelletto when cooked as follows: Cook the beans in water and remove them dry. Place oil and a few sage leaves in a pot. When the oil sizzles strongly, add the beans, season them with salt and pepper. Allow them to fry till they have absorbed the oil. Turn them over very often so that they cook evenly. Add some plain tomato sauce and when this has cooked well, remove the beans from the fire. These beans are to be served as a side dish to boiled meats unless they are served as a main dish.

238 — LOOSE FRESH BEANS AS A SIDE DISH TO BOILED MEAT

Loose beans, 11 ounces
Piece of dry meat, 1 ounce
Water, ½ pint
Oil, 4 spoonfuls
Sage leaves tied together, 4 or 5
Salt and white pepper

Place all the ingredients on the fire, allow them to boil slowly and stir often. Remove the sage leaves and the dry meat, and serve. This is usually enough for four servings.

239 — STRING BEANS PIE

Remove the ends and strings from a pound of beans. Throw them into boiling water with a pinch of salt, and as the water begins to boil again, remove the beans dry and place them in cold water. If you have meat gravy, flavor the string beans with it by placing them on the fire for a short time. Beans may also be flavored with a fricassee made with a quarter of an onion, some parsley, a piece of celery and oil, as follows: When the onion has browned, add the string beans, season them with salt and pepper, add as much water as necessary and allow them to boil slowly till done.

Prepare a sauce with 1 ounce of butter, a spoonful of flour and 1 pint of milk. Let the string beans get cold. Smear a dish with butter and cover the bottom with wax paper. Beat four eggs, mix them with a pinch of Parmesan cheese and the sauce; then mix the whole with the beans. Place the compound in a dish already prepared, and cook it either on the fire or in a double boiler. Serve hot.

240 — CAULIFLOWER PIE

Cauliflower, 12 or 13 ounces
Milk, ½ pint
Eggs, 3
Butter, 2 ounces
Grated Parmesan cheese, 1 ounce

Clean and boil the head of cauliflower, whole, till it is half done. Cut it into pieces. Fry it in half of the butter, stirring often, and when it has absorbed the butter, add a little of the milk and allow it to cook. Now either pass it through a sieve or leave it as it is. Make a sauce with the remainder of the butter, milk and a spoonful of flour. Add the beaten eggs and Parmesan and mix it with the cauliflower. Cook it in a smooth dish as for the String Beans Pie and serve hot.

This is usually sufficient for six servings.

241 — SPINACH PIE

Boil the spinach in very little water, or just in its own water. Pass it through a sieve, season it with salt, pepper and powdered cinnamon, two spoonfuls of any agreeable white sauce, butter, eggs, Parmesan cheese, and a pinch of raisins without seeds. Mix well and place the compound in a smooth dish with a hole in the middle and cook it in a double boiler. Remove it from the fire and serve hot with either chicken liver gravy or with a gravy made of milk-fed veal. If preferred, the gravy may be mixed with mushrooms.

242 — ARTICHOKE PIE

Remove the toughest leaves, cut the tips and peel the stems without cutting them. Cut the artichokes in four parts lengthwise and boil them in salted water for five minutes, and no longer, to assure a better taste. Remove them dry, mash them in a mortar and pass them through a sieve. Flavor with all the ingredients used in other vegetable pies, namely: eggs two or three spoonfuls of white sauce, abundant butter, Parmesan cheese, salt and nutmeg. Cook this compound in a double boiler in a dish with a hole in the middle if you have a meat gravy to fill it; otherwise, place it in a plain pie dish. Serve as a side dish.

243 — FINOCCHI (*Fennel*) PIE

Due to the flavor of fennel, this dish is a very savory one. Remove the hardest leaves from the fennel, cut it into pieces and boil it only ⅔ done in salted water. Strain the water and fry the fennel in butter. Season it with salt and pepper and when the butter has been absorbed, add some white sauce. Remove it from the fire, and if preferred, pass it through a sieve. When cold, add some grated Parmesan cheese and three or four beaten eggs. Pour this compound into a smooth dish. Cook it either in double boiler style and serve it as a side dish or use it with boiled capon. If preferred, it may be served with chicken liver.

244 — FRIED MUSHROOMS

It is advisable to use medium sized mushrooms. The large ones are too pulpy and the small ones are too hard. Scrape the stem, remove all the sand. Do not soak them; just wash them thoroughly. Cut them into slices as large as possible, dip them in flour and place them in frying oil, the best fat to use for this dish. Season with salt and pepper when about to remove them from the fire.

245 — STEWED MUSHROOMS

For a mushroom stew the small ones are to be preferred. Scrape and clean them as in the preceding recipe. When the oil, a clove of garlic and a pinch of catmint (catnip) are sizzling, add the mushrooms. Season with salt and pepper and when half cooked, add some tomato sauce.

246 — TRIPED MUSHROOMS

For this recipe, choose oval-shaped mushrooms. These are yellowish. When young, they are closed up in an egg-like shape, and when ripe, they open up and flatten out. The mushrooms are called triped because the treatment applied to them is the same as that for tripe. Cut them into thin slices after they are scraped and cleaned of sand. While cooking them in butter, add salt, pepper and grated Parmesan. A little meat gravy makes them very savory.

247 — GRIDDLED MUSHROOMS

The flattened oval shaped mushrooms are preferable for griddling. After having scraped and washed them, dry them between the folds of a canvas towel; season with oil, salt and pepper, and griddle them. Serve them as a side dish with any roast meat steak.

248 — DRY MUSHROOMS

Every year in September when mushrooms are cheap, one can preserve enough of them for winter provision. For this procedure, much sunshine is necessary. Young mushrooms are preferable. These are hard and small. One may make use of the large ones if they are not spongy. Scrape the stem, remove the sand thoroughly and cut them into large slices. If there are any worms in the stem, cut off only the part affected. Keep the mushrooms in the sun for two or three days; then string them up and keep them in a well ventilated room, and again in the sun till they are well dried. Place these dry mushrooms either in a carton or a paper bag. Look at them from time to time; if they are soft, air them for a while. This has to be done often to avoid moulding.

Before cooking, soak them in warm water for a very short time to prevent the loss of flavor. If your budget permits you to dry mushrooms in June, the result will be more satisfactory.

249 — EGG PLANT

Eggplant is a tasty and digestible vegetable, and a light one. It can be used as a side dish or as a regular course. When its natural bitter taste is slight, the egg plant makes a delicious dish. The small or medium sized plant is to be preferred, as the large ripe ones are likely to be bitter.

250 — FRIED EGG PLANT

Peel off the skin of the egg plant and cut it into small pieces; salt it and allow it to rest for an hour. Remove the water which has oozed out, dip the eggplant in flour, and fry it in oil.

251 — STEWED EGG PLANT

Peel the egg plant, cut it into small pieces and place it on the fire with a piece of butter. When the butter has been absorbed, add tomato sauce No. 78 and allow to cook.

252 — GRIDDLED EGG PLANT

Cut the egg plant lengthwise without peeling it. Make square-like incisions on the white part of the egg plant, add salt, pepper and oil and place it on the griddle with the skin underneath. Cover either with enameled or iron pot cover, and cook between two fires. When half done, add a little oil. When the pulp has become soft, it is done.

Fried egg plant is served as a side dish with fried fish. Stewed egg plant goes with boiled meat. Griddled egg plant is delicious with steak, veal cutlets or any roast meat.

253 — EGG PLANT PIE

Peel six or seven plants; cut them into round slices and salt them so as to allow them to ooze water for an hour. Dry them, cover them with flour and fry them in oil. Using a baking dish, place the egg plant in it in layers, seasoning each layer with grated Parmesan and tomato sauce No. 78. Beat an egg, add a pinch of salt, a spoonful of Parmesan cheese, two spoonfuls of grated bread and cover the surface of the egg plant with it. Place the dish in a country oven and when the egg has glazed, serve the egg plant pie. It can be used as a side dish with meat.

254 — BITTER-SWEET SCALLIONS

This is a simple dish. Peel the scallions, remove the green part, and place them in salted boiling water for a short time. If the amount of scallions is about 12 ounces, place 1 ounce of sugar in a dry pot and allow it to melt; add ½ ounce of flour and stir constantly. When the mixture has become red, pour in little by little, ⅔ of a glass of water mixed with vinegar, stir, and allow to boil till all froth disappear. Add the scallions and shake the pan often, but do not touch them with any utensil. Taste before serving, and add sugar or vinegar if necessary.

255 — STEWED SCALLIONS

Peel the scallions, remove the heads down to the white part, and cut off the lower end. Allow them to boil for ten minutes. Place a pan with a piece of butter on the fire, and as soon as it becomes dark brown, spread the scallions on it in a single layer. Season them with salt and pepper and allow them to brown evenly all around. Add some meat gravy and bind them with flour made into a paste with a piece of butter.

If you do not have meat gravy, cook the scallions as follows: After the scallions have been boiled and kept in cold water, place them in a pan with a bunch of aromatic herbs, a small slice of ham, a piece of butter and a ladle of stock soup. Season with salt and pepper, cover the whole with very thin slices of lardoı, and place a sheet of paper with butter spread on it on top. Allow them to cook between two fires and serve them with their own gravy.

256 — SIDE DISH OF CELERY

The ancients at the banquet table followed the custom of crowning their heads with celery, believing that this would neutralize the fumes of wine. Due to its delicate aroma, celery is tasty. It deserves to be placed among the health vegetables. Choose one with the thick stalks; the white part is the tenderest.

Here are three ways of cooking celery: For the first two it is suggested that the length of each stalk be 3 inches, while for the third $1\frac{1}{2}$ inches is sufficient. Clean the stalk and cut the lower part crosswise. Allow it to boil five minutes and remove it from the water dry.

1st: Fry the celery in butter, add some meat gravy and allow it to cook. Add some Parmesan cheese and serve.

2nd: For $\frac{1}{2}$ lb. of raw celery make a fricassee with 1 ounce of ham and a quarter of a medium sized onion. Chop finely. Place the fricassee in a pan with 1 ounce of butter, add two cloves and allow it to boil. When the onion has browned add some stock soup and continue cooking. Then pass it all through a sieve and pour this gravy on the celery which you have previously arranged in layers in a dish. Season with pepper and serve.

3rd: Dip the celery in flour, then cover it with

sauce No. 96, and fry it either in lard or oil. Or. if preferred, and this is even better, after covering it with flour, dip it into an egg, then cover it with grated bread and fry. Celery cooked in this style makes a savory side dish with stewed meats.

257 — WHOLE LENTILS AS A SIDE-DISH

After the lentils have been cooked, add butter and meat gravy to them as seasoning. If this is not available, cook them together with a bunch of aromatic herbs and drain the water from them. Make a fricassee of lean and fat ham, a bit of butter and a little onion. When it is well browned, pour in one or two tablespoon of the strained broth of the sausage or of the zampone which is being used as the main dish. Let it boil for a while, strain it, and cook the lentils in this mixture, adding butter, salt and pepper.

258 — ARTICHOKES WITH GRAVY

Remove the hard leaves, cut off the tips and peel the skin from the stalk. Cut the artichokes into four pieces or into six if they are large. Set them on the fire with sufficient butter, and season with salt and pepper. Shake the pan so that the pieces do not burn, and cook them evenly all around. As soon as most of the butter has been absorbed, add enough stock soup and continue cooking. Remove them dry.

Cut a few parsley leaves finely and add them to the gravy with a spoonful of grated bread and some lemon juice; beat everything and allow it to boil a short time. Add salt and pepper to suit your taste.

Remove the gravy from the fire, and when it has stopped boiling, add one or two egg yolks and more stock soup. Replace it on the fire and mix well. Add the artichokes so as to warm them up and serve them as a side dish to boiled meats.

259 — ARTICHOKES RITTI
(Cooked straight up)

This is the name which the Florentines give to the artichokes when cooked in the following simple manner:

Remove the small leaves from the stalk and cut off the stalk. Cut the tips of the leaves and open the inside leaves as wide as possible. Place the artichokes standing in a pot together with the peeled stalks whole. Season with salt, pepper and oil in good measure. Cover and allow to fry. When browned, add a little water and allow them to cook.

260 — ARTICHOKES STUFFED WITH MEAT

For six artichokes make the following stuffing:

Lean milk-fed veal, 3½ ounces
Ham (more fat than lean), 1 ounce
Cores of artichokes
New onion, ¼
A few leaves of parsley
Dry mushrooms, soaked in water, ½ doz
A slice of white bread, cut into pieces
A pinch of grated Parmesan cheese
Salt, pepper and some spices

Mix well; fill the artichokes with the stuffing, and set them to brown in a pot with some oil, adding a little water. Cover the pot with a clean wet white cloth and place the cover on it to keep it tight. The vapor issuing from the artichokes will surround and cook them evenly, and they will taste better.

261 — STUFFED ARTICHOKES

Cut the stalk of the artichokes at the bottom, remove the outside leaves and wash them. Cut off the tips from the leaves and open the inner leaves wide enough to cut off the core with a small knife. Save the small tender leaves of the core for stuffing. For six artichokes prepare the following stuffing:

Ham (more fat than lean), 2 ounces
¼ new onion
A piece of garlic, the size of the tip of a finger
A leaf of celery and of parsley and the leaves of the cores
Half a dozen dry mushrooms, soaked in water
A slice of white bread, cut into small pieces
Salt and pepper

Cut the ham into pieces; chop all the ingredients with a chopper; stuff the artichokes and cook them as described in the preceding recipe.

262 — GRILLED ARTICHOKES

These artichokes are to be used as a side dish with steak or meat roast. Use only tender artichokes. Cut off the tips of the leaves, and cut the stalks at the base. Do not remove any of the leaves. Open the leaves wide enough to retain seasoning of oil, salt and pepper. Place the artichokes straight up on the griddle to broil. When half done, baste them with oil without removing them from the fire, and leave them on the fire till outside leaves are charred.

263 — DRY ARTICHOKES PRESERVED FOR WINTER

This is done in places where artichokes are not found the year round. It is not necessary in warm regions where they are abundant all the time.

It is advisable to preserve them at the height of the season, when they are less expensive, and they are ripe. Remove the hard leaves, cut the tips of the leaves and cut the stalks at the base. Then split the artichokes into four parts, removing all visible fuzz. As they are cut, throw them into cool water containing either vinegar or lemon juice to prevent them from turning black. Place them in an earthen pot in boiling water, add a little bunch of aromatic herbs, consisting of basil, celery leaves, thyme etc. and allow them to boil ten minutes or less, as they can be removed half done. Drain the water and spread them out on a flat dish to dry in the sun. After a while string them up and finish drying them in a well ventilated and shady place. It is not advisable to keep them in the sun too long, as they may get the odor of hay. When frying them as a side dish, soak them in water first.

264 — PEAS I.

This is a recipe for one quart of loose fresh peas. Cut two new onions in half lengthwise; place a few sprigs of parsley between them and tie them up. Place these onions on the fire with a little over 1 ounce of butter and brown them. Add a large ladleful of stock soup, and allow them to boil till they are well done. Pass the onions through a sieve together with the soup by squeezing them. Replace the soup in a pot with the peas and two hearts of lettuce. Season with salt and pepper and boil slowly. When half done, add 1 ounce of butter mixed with a tablespoonful of flour, adding more soup, it necessary. Before serving, bind the peas with two egg yolks diluted in a little soup. This is a very savory dish.

265 — PEAS II.

The preparation of this dish is simpler than the preceding one but it is less tasty. Slice some onions very fine and place them in a pot with a piece of butter. When browned, add a pinch of flour, mix well and add, according to the quantity, one or two ladlefuls of stock soup. Allow the flour to cook and add the peas, seasoning with salt and pepper. When half done, add two whole hearts of lettuce. Boil slowly and see that the gravy does not thicken too much. Some people prefer to add sugar, but it is advisable to use very little of it if the natural sweetness of the peas is to be preserved. When serving, remove the lettuce.

266 — PEAS WITH SMOKED HAM

The restaurant cooks of Rome prepare the most tasty cooked peas, not because the peas grown in the soil around Rome are of such excellent or superior quality, but because they are seasoned with smoked ham.

Cut lengthwise, proportionate to the quantity of peas, one or two new onions and fry them in oil with some smoked diced ham, both lean and fat. Fry till the ham shrinks and add the peas. Season with very little salt and some pepper; mix well, add stock soup and boil slowly, adding a piece of butter.

267 — PEAS WITH DRY MEAT

Fry some chopped dry meat, garlic and parsley together in oil; season with salt and pepper, and as soon as the garlic becomes brown, add the peas. As the fat is absorbed, add either some stock soup or water and boil slowly till done.

268 — CAULIFLOWER WITH BALSAMELLA
(White Sauce)

Remove the green and white leaves from a large head, cut the stalk crosswise, rather deeply, and boil the cauliflower in salt water till done. Cut it in small slices and let it take on flavor with butter, salt and pepper. Place it in an oven-proof dish, sprinkle with Parmesan cheese, and cover it with the following balsamella (white sauce) prepared simultaneously with the cauliflower:

Place a spoonful of flour with a piece of butter as large as an egg on the fire. Mix well when light brown, pour in a pint of milk, little by little. Stir steadily till it is condensed into a milky cream-like liquid. If this balsamella is too thick, place it on the fire again with another pieces of butter mixed with flour to thin the sauce.

Place the dish of caufiflower with the white sauce over it in the oven, leaving it there till the seasoning has flavored the vegetable, and serve it either as a second course or as a side dish with meat or boiled fowl.

269 — SAUERKRAUT I.

This is an imitation of the German Sauerkraut and can be used as a side-dish to sausages, zamponi, or simple stew.

Take a head of white cabbage, remove the green leaves and cut it into four parts, starting at the stem. Wash them in fresh water and slice them very finely crosswise. Now put the cabbage in an earthenware pot, salt it, and pour boiling water on it until it is covered. When it is cold, remove it, pressing it out well; put it in the pot again with a bit of strong vinegar mixed in a glass of water. Leave it in this way for several hours; press it out well, and cook it in the following way:

Chop finely, a slice of fat ham or of dry meat and put it in a casserole with a piece of butter; when it is browned throw in the cabbage and cook it with broth of sausage or of zampone if it is not too spicy. Taste the sauerkraut for vinegar and salt.

270 — SAUERKRAUT II.

Take a head of white or of green cabbage, cut it into strips about ½ inch wide and keep it in fresh water. Remove it from the water without squeezing it out, and put it on the fire to ooze water. Make a fricassee with ¼ of an onion, a bit of finely chopped dry meat and some butter. When it has taken on color, throw in the cabbage together with a piece of dry meat, which is removed later. Season with salt and pepper.

Boil slowly, adding broth, and in the end add a bit of vinegar and a teaspoon of sugar.

271 — BROCCOLI OR TALLI DI RAPE IN FLORENTINE STYLE

Broccoli di rape are simply leaves picked together with the tufts, or, a rather long and thin stalk bearing small seeded broccoli sprouts. It is a healthy vegetable, very popular in Tuscany, but on account of its bitter taste, it is not appreciated in other regions of Italy, and even the poor dislike it.

Remove the tough leaves, boil the broccoli, strain the water and cut them into rather large pieces. Either chop or leave whole two or three cloves of garlic and fry them in a pan with abundant oil. As the garlic browns, add the broccoli, seasoning them with salt and pepper, turning them often, and frying them for a considerable time. This dish can be served either as a course or a side dish, with boiled meat. If fine oil is not available, lard can be substituted.

272 — STUFFED CABBAGE

Remove the rough outer leaves from a large head of cabbage, cut the stalk even with the leaves and boil it in salted water until half done.

The stuffing is prepared either simply with milk-fed veal, boiled till over-done, or combined with lamb's liver, chopped finely. Season the stuffing with white sauce, a pinch of Parmesan cheese, an egg yolk and flavor of nutmeg.

Now open the leaves one by one till the core is reached and pour the stuffing on it; close up the leaves with the stuffing as tightly as possible, and tie the cabbage crosswise. Place the cabbage in the soup-like gravy left from the previously-boiled veal (used for stuffing), add a small piece of butter and cook it in the oven on a low fire. If preferred, the large leaves of the cabbage can be stuffed, one by one, and rolled to form "vegetable and meat rolls".

273 — WHITE CABBAGE AS A SIDE DISH

Cut a head of white cabbage into four parts from the stalk, and each of these parts into small slices. Soak it in fresh water, then dip it for a short time in boiling salted water. Remove it from the fire and drain the water without squeezing.

Chop a piece of ham and some onion together, and fry them in butter. As the onion browns, add a ladleful of stock soup, boil it for a while and pass the soup through a sieve. Place this soup, the cabbage and a slice of ham in a pot, season with a little salt and pepper and cook on a low fire. Remove the ham, and serve the cabbage as a side dish with boiled meat.

274 — SIDE DISH OF BLACK CABBAGE

Remove the hard leaves from a head of black cabbage, boil it and slice it finely. Instead of meat gravy, chop some ham and onion and fry it in butter. As the onion browns, add some stock soup, boil a short while, and pass the gravy through a fine sieve. Place the cabbage in this gravy, season it with salt and pepper, adding more stock soup and a piece of butter, if necessary. Serve with pigs knuckles or any boiled meat.

275 — FENNEL WITH WHITE SAUCE

Choose meaty fennel; remove the tough leaves and slice the fennel rather thinly. Wash it, and boil it in salted water for a short time. Fry in butter, When it has absorbed the butter, add sufficient milk and cook. After tasting for seasoning, remove it dry and place it in a baking dish. Sprinkle with Parmesan cheese and cover with balsamella (white sauce). Bake in the oven for a while, and serve either with boiled or baked meat.

276 — FENNEL AS A SIDE-DISH

This recipe is simpler than the preceding one.
Cut the fennel into pieces, scald it in salted water, fry it in butter, cook with broth, add a bit of flour. Season the fennel with Parmesan on removing it from the fire.

277 — POTATO SAUTE'

In plain language, this means potatoes fried in butter. Peel the potatoes and slice them thinly. Place them in a frying pan with butter, seasoning with salt and pepper. It is customary to place these potatoes under the steak when serving.

If preferred, the potatoes may be fried in oil, as follows: If cooking new potatoes, it is not necessary to peel them; rubbing with a thick cloth will remove the thin skin. Cut them in thin slices and soak them in fresh water for an hour. Dry them in canvas cloth, cover the slices with flour, and fry them in oil till not too well done. Salt when ready and serve.

278 — TRUFFLED POTATOES

Slice some boiled potatoes thinly when only half done. Place the slices in layers in a pie dish, alternating with a layer of truffles, also thinly sliced and sprinkled with Parmesan. Add a piece of butter, season with salt and pepper; and as soon as they sizzle, add a little stock soup or meat gravy. Before removing them from the fire, squeeze a few drops of lemon juice on them, and serve them warm.

279 — TORTINO OF YOUNG SQUASH

Cut the young squash in pieces as large as nuts, fry it in butter till brown and season with salt and pepper. Place it in a baking dish, sprinkle with Parmesan cheese mixed with a little nutmeg, and cover it with a large, thick balsamella or white sauce Bake it in the oven under the fire to allow the surface to brown. Serve with boiled or stewed meat.

280 — SPINACH AS A SIDE DISH

Stew and chop the spinach finely. After this preliminary step, spinach can be cooked in any of the following ways.

1) With butter, salt and pepper, adding a little meat gravy, or broth, or even cream.
2) With a little fricassee of onion finely chopped and fried in butter.
3) With butter, salt and pepper, adding a pinch of Parmesan.
4) With butter, a drop of oil, and tomato sauce.

281 — SPINACH IN THE STYLE OF ROMAGNA

Stew the spinach in the water which it oozes. Remove it dry and put it in a fricassee of oil, garlic, parsley, salt and pepper. Do not break the spinach stalks and season with a bit of sugar and some seedless raisins.

282 — ASPARAGI

First scrape the white part of the asparagi with a knife and cut off the hard part. The water should be boiling strongly (bubbling) before the asparagi are placed in it. Salt the water before placing the asparagi in it to keep them green. When the asparagi bend their heads, they are done. When they give way to a moderate finger-pressure, it is also a sign that they are cooked. It is best not to allow them to become too soft. Remove them with a perforated ladle, putting them into fresh water for a short time, but remove them quickly so as to serve them warm.

After the asparagi are boiled, they may be seasoned in various ways. The simplest way is to season them with fine olive oil and vinegar or lemon juice. but here are a few other ways of preparing this tasty vegetable:

1) Fry the asparagi in butter, and serve.
2) Season them with salt and pepper, and a pinch of Parmesan cheese. Pour on some fried butter when it is about to brown.
3) Cut the white from the green parts, and prepare as follows: Sprinkle some Parmesan cheese in a baking dish. Make a layer of asparagus tips, season with salt and pepper, Parmesan cheese and small pieces of butter. Make another layer crosswise and add some seasoning, repeating the operation until all the vegetable is used up. Do not season them too strongly, as this may spoil the taste of the asparagi. Cook them over a fire or in the oven unti! they have taken on flavor, and serve them warm
4) If meat gravy is available, boil the asparagi half done. and finish cooking them in the gravy.

These are the simplest and most wholesome ways to prepare this healthy vegetable.

283 — YOUNG SQUASH PIE

Young squash, 1½ lbs.
Parmesan cheese. 1½ ounces
Eggs, 4
Onion, one fourth
Celery, carrot, parsley

Chop together the onion, celery, carrot and parsley. Fry them in oil till brown, and add the young squash, which has been cut into small pieces and seasoned with salt and pepper. When browned, add sufficient water and cook. When done, pass it through a sieve and add the eggs and the Parmesan. Mix well.

Make a balsamella (white sauce) with 2 ounces of butter, 2 tablespoons of flour and a pint of milk. Add this to the compound and mix till everything is blended.

Make a hole in the middle of the pie and cook it in a double boiler. Remove it while warm, fill the center hole with a choice delicate sauce and serve.

This quantity is sufficient for eight or ten people.

284 — MUSHROOM PIE

Use a little over a pound of fresh mushrooms.

Medium size mushrooms are preferable Remove all visible sand and wash them thoroughly. Cut them into pieces as large as peas. Place them on the fire with salt and pepper, and when half done add enough meat gravy and cook. Remove them from the fire and bind them with a balsamella made of eggs and Parmesan cheese, and allow them to condense while cooking in a double boiler.

1½ lbs. of mushrooms and 5 eggs would make a pie to serve ten people. Serve warm as entree.

285 — GREEN CABBAGE AS A SIDE-DISH

Stew the cabbage till it is half-done, remove it dry, chop it and put it on the fire with butter and milk to cook it. When it is well cooked, add some rather thick balsamella sauce. Leave the cabbage on the fire a while longer and add grated Parmesan cheese.

Serve as a side-dish for any stewed or boiled meats.

FISH DISHES
286 — CACCIUCCO I.

The word "cacciucco" simply means gravy, but it is a name by which the Florentines call any fish prepared in this particular style.

This recipe requires 2 pounds of fish. Cut half an onion finely and fry it in oil, adding parsley and two whole cloves of garlic. As soon as the onion takes on color, add ¾ pounds of fresh tomatoes diced or canned tomato sauce, and ½ inch of a wine-glass of strong vinegar diluted in a glassful of water. Boil for a minute or so, remove the garlic and pass the tomato through a sieve, squeezing it well. Place the sauce on the fire again together with the fish, which will have been prepared by this time. This fish may be any choice of filet of sole, mullet, dog salmon, shrimps, or any other fish in season. If it is a large fish cut it into pieces. Taste the gravy for seasoning, and add a little oil if necessary. When the fish is cooked, and the cacciucco (gravy) has the desired taste, serve in two separate dishes: one with the fish without gravy, and another containing slices of white bread, ½ inch thick, to be dipped in the left over cacciucco.

287 — CACCIUCCO II.

This is a cacciucco prepared at Viareggio. It is less succulent than the previous one, but more digestible. For the same quantity of fish, chop three cloves of garlic and some zenzero (fresh or dry) red hot pepper in a mortar until it is reduced to powder. Place it in an earthen pot with sufficient oil on the fire and when browned, add a glass of liquid consisting of $\frac{1}{3}$ of a glass of dry white wine and $\frac{2}{3}$ of water. Place the fish in this gravy, cook for a short while, then add tomato sauce or tomato paste diluted in water, and boil rapidly, with the pot covered. Do not turn the fish to avoid breaking it; it will cook in a few minutes.

Serve with toast in same manner as for the preceding recipe.

288 — FISH AL PIATTO
(Cooked in a special flat dish)

It is known that fish is not a very nourishing food, and therefore it is advisable to eat it as an entree with meat dishes to balance the meal. For this special fish course, use either a small fish or thin cuts of a large fish. If filet of sole and mullet are chosen, cut the filet into three small pieces, clean and wash them very thoroughly, and arrange the pieces in a smooth metal dish. Season with chopped garlic, parsley, salt, pepper, oil, a few drops of lemon juice, and some fine white wine. Spread on top, as well as under the fish, some chopped garlic and parsley, pour in more oil and more of the ingredients mentioned above, in such abundance that the fish wades in oil. Cook it in the oven, both above and under the fire. It is a palatable dish to serve at family dinners.

289 — BOILED FISH

Place sufficient salted water on the fire. and before putting in the fish, boil it for 15 minutes with ¼ of an onion stuck with two cloves of garlic. pieces of celery stalks, carrot. parsley, and two or three thin slices of lemon.

When the eyes of the fish seem to pop out, the fish is done. Another sign is that the skin falls apart as soon as touched. Serve the fish warm with a little of the water in which it was boiled and trimmed with parsley, beets, finely sliced boiled potatoes. and slices of hard-boiled eggs.

290 — FISH CUTS WITH GRAVY

Cuts from tuna fish, grayling, seawolf, bass, sturgeon, etc. may be used. 1½ pounds ought to be sufficient for five servings.

Remove the scales, wash the fish well and dry it. Cover it with flour and brown it in oil. Remove the fish dry discarding the oil residue, and clean the pan. Chop finely ½ onion, a piece of celery about 10 inches long and a generous sprig of parsley. Place this on the fire with abundant oil, seasoning with salt, pepper and a bit of clove. When it has taken on color, add sufficient tomato sauce and boil for a while. Place the fish in this sauce and cook it to taste, turning it around often while cooking. Serve fish in its own gravy.

291 — NASELLO PALERMO STYLE
(Fresh Cod Fish)

Cut off all the fins except those of the tail of a fresh cod fish weighing about 1½ pounds Do not remove the head. Open the front, removing the interior and the backbone; flatten it and season it with salt and pepper. Turn the fish back up, moisten it with oil, add salt and pepper, and cover it with grated stale bread. Place it in a baking dish with the back up.

Clean 3 anchovies of scales and bones, chop them finely and melt them on the fire in a spoonful of oil, but do not boil them. Put this sauce on the back of the fish and cover it with grated stale bread. Add some rosemary leaves and cook it in the oven, over and then under the fire until a brownish crust is formed. Moisten with a little oil and squeeze half a lemon on it.

This is sufficient for four or five servings with buttered, anchovied or caviar toast.

292 — SOLE ON THE GRIDIRON OR FRIED

To bring out the flavor it is advisable to cook a large sole on the grate and season it with lard instead of oil.

Scrape off all the scales, wash the fish, clean it and dry it thoroughly in a canvas cloth. Smear the fish with cold, virgin lard, add salt and pepper, and cover it with bread crumbs. Melt a little lard in a small pot and spread it on the fish again with a clean feather. Place the filet on the griddle, and turn it over while broiling, smearing it with the lardy feather till done.

To fry a sole of large size, skin the fish on both sides, dip it, first in flour, then in beaten egg and keep it there for an hour before placing it in a hot frying pan.

Filet of sole is a delicate fish so much so that the French people call it sea-partridge in appreciation of its delicacy.

293 — FILET OF SOLE WITH WINE

Choose soles weighing at least six ounces each. Wash the heads and remove all the skin. With a sharp knife separate the bones from the flesh, making four large strips or slices from each fish. Flatten the slices first with the handle of the knife, then with a blade till they become as thin as possible but are still intact. Leave them in beaten eggs, seasoned with salt and pepper, for a few hours. Dip them in grated stale bread and fry them in oil. Place the filets in a baking dish with a little of the oil in which they were fried, add a piece of butter, season with salt and pepper again, and bake for a short time. Add some dry white wine and chopped parsley, and cook for about five minutes more. Sprinkle with Parmesan cheese and serve the fish in its own gravy.

294 — MULLETS ON THE GRIDIRON
SAILOR STYLE

Remove the inner part from the gills with a short knife; wash the mullets thoroughly and dry them well. Place a piece of garlic in the gills, season with salt and pepper, oil, rosemary leaves and allow to rest for a while. When about to broil, dip the fish in grated stale bread, and while on the grate, smear it with oil. Serve with lemon slices at the side.

295 — MULLETS, LEGHORN STYLE

Chop some garlic, parsley and a piece of celery together and fry it in oil. As the garlic takes on color, add sliced tomatoes and season with salt and pepper. Cook the sauce well, stirring often; then strain the sauce thoroughly, squeezing the tomato. Smear a deep baking dish with oil, put the mullets into it, and as the oil sizzles, cover them with the tomato sauce already prepared and cook them in it. Be sure that the dish is deep enough and the sauce covers the fish so that it is not necessary to turn it.

Before removing it from the fire, spread some chopped parsley on the surface, and serve. The months of September and October are the season for mullets.

296 — LOBSTER

A sign of good quality in lobsters is when their weight is proportionate to their size. It is desirable to purchase them when alive, or at least, when they still give sign of life. First, tie the tail to the lower part of the body and throw the lobster into boiling water, already flavored by having boiled in it a bunch of aromatic herbs consisting of an onion, carrot, parsley and bay leaves. Add one or two spoonfuls of vinegar, a pinch of salt, and boil from 30 to 40 minutes, according to the size of the lobster. Allow the lobster to cool off in its own water, then dry it thoroughly. Smear a few drops of oil on it to give it lustre Cut it from head to tail so that the pulp can be easily removed from the shell and serve either with oil and lemon juice or with mayonnaise.

Another savory sauce can be made in the following manner: Remove the pulp from the head of the lobster, chop it together with a hard-boiled egg and some parsley. Place this compound in a sauce dish, season it with pepper an a very little salt, and dilute it with fine olive oil and the juice of half a lemon or vinegar. This is a very palatable sauce.

297 — EELS, FLORENTINE STYLE

Remove the skin by making a circular incision just below the head. Hold the head tightly between the folds of a canvas towel and pull off the skin. Cut the eel into pieces about three inches long, season it with oil, salt and pepper, and allow it to rest for an hour or two.

Place the fish in a metal dish with oil, two cloves of garlic (not cut), some sage leaves, and fry it for a short time. Remove the pieces one by one, dip in grated bread and place them in a row in a baking dish, pouring the oil left from the former frying on them.

Cook above and below the flame, and when the fish has taken on color, pour in a little water. Due to its oily meat, this fish is rather heavy for the stomach.

298 — EELS WITH SAUCE

For this dish large eels are to be preferred. Cut them into short pieces without removing the skin. Chop a large onion together with plenty of parsley and fry it in oil. Season with salt and pepper, and as soon as the onion has browned, add the eels. As soon as the oil has been absorbed, add tomato sauce or tomato paste diluted in water. Boil slowly in abundant sauce if you wish to serve it on toast. This is a delicate dish, though not digestible for everybody.

299 — FISH CAKE

The following ingredients are sufficient to prepare a cake for 12 servings:

Fish, any kind preferred, 1 lb.
Rice, 7 ounces
Fresh peas, 12 ounces
Fresh mushrooms, 7 ounces
Toasted Pine seeds, 1½ ounces
Butter; Parmesan cheese
Artichokes, 6
Eggs, 2

Boil the rice in 1½ ounces of butter and ¼ of a chopped onion. Salt it, and when done, bind it with eggs and Parmesan cheese.

Chop and fry in butter some onion, celery, carrot and parsley. Boil the mushrooms and artichokes till half done, add them to the fried herbs and cook them, adding one or two spoonfuls of warm water. Season with salt, pepper and 1½ ounces of Parmesan after they are removed from the fire.

Chop some garlic and parsley, and fry it in oil, add tomato sauce, salt and pepper. Cook the fish which has been sliced in this sauce.When done, remove the fish, strain the gravy and add the toasted Pine seeds (which have been ground in a mortar) to it. Now remove the head and the bones from the fish and mix everything together, except the rice.

When all the ingredients of the fish pie are ready, make the crust with the following:

Flour, 1 lb.
Butter, 2½ ounces
White marsala wine, 2 tablespoons
Salt
2 Eggs

Smear a pie dish with butter, cover it with pie crust, and pour half of the rice on the crust, spreading it evenly. Add the entire stuffing and then the remainder of the rice. Cover it with the pie crust and bake. When done, remove it from the pie dish and serve either warm or cold.

300 — BACCALA, FLORENTINE STYLE
(Dry Cod Fish)

If you buy the baccala dry, soak it in fresh water for at least one day, changing the water at least four times. Cut the baccala into pieces as large as a hand, and dip them in flour. Flatten two or three cloves of garlic and fry them whole in abundant oil. When the garlic becomes brown, put in the baccala and brown it evenly on both sides. Turn the fish often to avoid sticking. Add a pinch of pepper and a few spoonfuls of tomato paste diluted in water. Cook a while longer and serve.

301 — BACCALA, BOLOGNESE STYLE

After soaking the baccala as described in the preceding recipe, cut the fish into pieces. Place it in a pot smeared with oil, spread chopped garlic and parsley on it, adding a pinch of pepper, oil and a small piece of butter. Cook over a strong fire and turn the fish carefully to avoid breaking. When done, squeeze half a lemon on it and serve.

302 — BACCALA, BITTER-SWEET

Cook this as in the Florentine style, No. 300, but use less garlic. When the fish is browned on both sides, add the bitter-sweet prepared as follows: For 1½ pounds of baccala, put less than one inch of vinegar in a glass, add twice that much water, some sugar, Pine seeds and white currants. Boil this in a separate pot, and pour it on the baccala, served warm.

303 — GRILLED BACCALA

So that the baccala will be less dry, cook it with a low fire on a sheet of white paper smeared with butter. Season with oil, pepper and rosemary leaves, if desired.

304 — CUTLETS OF BACCALA

One must not expect much delicacy of taste from baccala, but if prepared in the following manner, it will prove an agreeable change.

Boil about 18 ounces of baccala. Chop it finely with two anchovies, some parsley, a pinch of pepper, a goodly pinch of grated Parmesan. Add 3 or 4 tablespoonfuls of filling, consisting of dry crustless bread, boiled in water, with some butter and two eggs. Mix well. Take one tablespoonful of this compound and dip it in grated bread, flatten it with the hand into a cutlet shape; then dip it in a beaten egg, and in grated bread again. Fry it in oil and serve it either with lemon slices at side or with tomato sauce.

ROASTS
305 — ROAST MILK-FED VEAL

Milk-fed veal is seasonal in Spring and Summer. because at that time it is tasty and tender. Loin of rump is the part which makes the best roast, as no seasoning is required when cooked on the grate, except a little oil and salt.

These same pieces, stuck with very little garlic and rosemary, can be pot-roasted, together with oil, butter, some chopped ham, salt, pepper and tomato sauce. If preferred, cook some fresh peas in the same gravy. It is an excellent dish.

306 — ARROSTO MORTO
(A sort of pot roast)

You may choose any meat you like for this roast. but milk-fed veal is very appropriate, especially that part of the loin which holds the kidney. Prepare and cook it as follows:

Tie the meat with a strong string and place it in a pot with a very small quantity of fine olive oil and a little butter, and let it brown on both sides. When half done, season with salt and add either some stock soup or tomato sauce. Cook slowly till the meat has absorbed a good deal of the sauce and very little gravy is left. If you like it spicy, add some chopped smoked ham or dry pork sausage in the beginning.

307 — ARROSTO MORTO SEASONED WITH GARLIC AND ROSEMARY LEAVES

Do not put too much garlic and rosemary in the meat. Whatever meat is chosen, the procedure is exactly the same as in the preceding recipe, except that only a clove of garlic and a few leaves of rosemary are added. Cook slowly, and when about to serve, strain the gravy, and serve with a side dish of potatoes or vegetables. Leg of lamb is a choice meat for this dish.

308 — ROAST OF BIRDS

Choose birds that are fat and be sure that they are fresh. Do not clean them before putting them on the spit, but arrange them in the following manner. Bend back the wings and insert one or two sage leaves between the wings and the back. Cut off the tips of the feet and cross them so that the knees meet; pierce the tendon and stick a sage leaf into it. Place them on the spit with the largest birds in the center; between the birds place bread crusts, about 1 inch wide.

Cover the breast of the bird with thin salted slices of lard, so that the spit passes both through the lard and through the birds.

When cooking them keep them with the head downward for a while, to lengthen the neck. Smear them with oil only once, when they begin to get brown, but do not touch the bread crusts. Salt them.

Do not cook them too long before the meal, so that they do not dry up. Remove them from the spit together and leave them lined up.

309 — LAMB ROAST ALL'ARETINA
(Aretina Style)

The time for lamb is from December to Easter time. Season a leg of lamb with salt, pepper, oil and a little vinegar. Make a cut or incision here and there with a short knife, filling the cuts with the seasoning. Allow it to rest several hours. Place the meat on the gridiron and broil it slowly white basting it with oil and vinegar by means of a bunch of rosemary leaves. This will eliminate that peculiar taste of lamb which, to some people, is intolerable.

310 — ROAST OF LEG OF MUTTON

Mutton is in season from October to May. It is said that the mutton with short legs and dark reddish meat is tastiest, in addition to being most wholesome. If freshly killed mutton is used, put it on ice for a couple of days to make it tender. When taken from the ice, beat it with a wooden mallet and remove the film and the center bone. Tie it up well, and place it on the gridirion or grate under a strong fire. When half done, lower the fire. As soon as it begins to ooze fat (which should be saved), baste it with the fat mixed with some fatless stock soup, till it is done. Season with salt when almost done. Do not cook too rare or too much. When serving, wrap the end bone of the leg with white waxed paper, fringed at the end, to lend the table a touch of decoration.

311 — ROAST OF HARE

The rear part of the hare is the most desirable for a roast of this kind. Remove all visible pellicles from the venison meat without cutting the meat itself.

Before putting it on the grate, place it in a solution prepared as follows: Place in a pot three glasses of water, about half a glass (more or less according to whether the meat is a small or a large piece) of vinegar, three or four diced scallions, a couple of laurel leaves, a small bunch of parsley and a pinch of salt and pepper. Boil for five or six minutes, and when cold, pour the solution on the rabbit meat. Allow the meat to remain in the liquid for 12 or 14 hours. Remove the meat, dry it well; then stick it with thin pieces of fine salt pork and broil it under a low fire. Season with salt and smear with milk cream. Some people believe that the liver of the hare should not be eaten.

312 — ARROSTO MORTO LARDELLATO

Choose a short and thick piece of lean milk-fed veal of about 2½ pounds, either from the leg or from the bottom round, and stick it in various places with 1 ounce of ham, both fat and lean, thinly sliced. Tie it well and place it in the oven with 1 ounce of butter, ¼ of an onion cut in two parts, 3 or 4 celery leafstalks about 4 inches long, and 3 or 4 thin slices of carrot. Season with salt and pepper. Turn the meat often to brown it evenly. Add 2 small ladlefuls of water and cook it over a low fire. Let the meat absorb most of the gravy, but take care that the meat does not become too dark. When about to serve it, pass the remaining gravy through a sieve and pour it on the roast. It is advisable to add a side dish of potatoes, sliced, and fried in butter.

313 — ROASTED STUFFED BEEF BRACIUOLA

For a braciuola of beef weighing 1¼ pounds, use the following ingredients:

Lean milk-fed veal, 8 ounces
Ham, lean and fat, 1 ounce
Salted tongue, 1 ounce
Grated Parmesan cheese, 1 ounce
Butter, 1 ounce (or more)
Chicken livers, 2
Egg, 1
Bread Crumbs, 1 cup

Chop together a small onion a piece of celery, a carrot and parsley. Fry this in butter, and as soon as the onion browns, add the veal and the chicken liver cut into small pieces. Season with salt and pepper and cook slowly, adding a little stock soup. Remove the veal and the liver, dry and chop it finely with a half-moon chopper. Mix it with the bread, egg, Parmesan cheese, the ham and tongue diced. Now that the stuffing is prepared, slice the beef, pass it through water so as to flatten it easily. First beat it well, extending it as much as possible, and then flatten it with a large knife blade. Place the stuffing in the middle and roll the meat as neatly as possible, tying it tightly lengthwise and crosswise like a salami. Place it on the grate and broil it, basting it with oil and salt.

This is a delicate roast, sufficient for six or seven servings.

314 — STUFFED CHICKEN

This is not a dish for fancy dinners, but wholesome family food. The following ingredients are for a medium-sized chicken:

Sausage, 2 pieces
1 chicken liver, crest and kidneys of the same fowl
Well-roasted chestnuts. 8 or 10
Truffle or dried mushroom, 1 piece
Egg, 1
Flavor of nutmeg

If instead of a chicken you wish to stuff a turkey, double the quantity of the above ingredients.

Fry the sausage, chicken liver, crest and kidneys

in butter, adding stock soup as needed. Season with very little salt and a pinch of pepper and remove dry when half done. Place a slice of white crustless bread in this gravy so as to obtain 2 tablespoons of hard mash. Peel the sausage, chop the chicken liver, etc. together with the soaked mushroom. Add the nuts, egg and mash, and mash them finely in a mortar. (If you are using the truffle, do not mix it in now, but cut it into thin slices and add it raw). This makes a fine stuffing. If the chicken is sliced when cold, it will make a tasty delicacy.

315 — RABBIT ROAST

Use the rear part of the rabbit for this roast. Wrap the meat in strips of lard, smear it with oil or butter and put it on the spit. Salt when almost done.

316 — CHICKEN IN DEVIL STYLE

It is called this way because the chicken should be seasoned with Cayenne pepper and a very spicy gravy, so that he who eats it is tempted to send the chicken and the cook to the devil. The following is a simpler recipe.

Take a young fowl, remove the neck and feet, open it along the breast, and flatten it as much as possible. Wash and dry it well; place it on the gridiron, turn it when it begins to get brown, smear it with butter or oil, and add salt and pepper. Turn it again and apply the same treatment. Continue this procedure until the chicken is cooked.

317 — POLLO IN PORCHETTA

(Chicken in the style of roast pig)

This is not a dish for guests, but it is good for the family.

Stuff a chicken with slices of fat and lean ham, as wide as a finger, add 3 whole cloves of garlic, some fennel and a grain of pepper. Season with salt and pepper and cook it with butter both above and beneath the fire. The ham can be substituted by sausages.

318 — GUINEA HEN

The best way to cook guinea-hens is to roast them on the spit. Put a ball of salted butter into the guinea-hens and wrap them in a sheet of paper smeared with butter and covered with salt. Remove the paper when the guinea hens are half-done, finish cooking them and let them take on color, basting them with oil and salting them.

319 — ROAST DUCK

Salt the inside of the duck. Tie thin, wide slices of salt pork with a string around its breast. Smear it with olive oil and set it in the oven. When done, salt it to taste. If it is a wild duck, use butter instead of olive oil, because butter is a heavier fat and better suitable for lean fowl.

320 — TURKEY

Turkey can be cooked in many ways: stewed, boiled, grilled and roasted. The broth of turkey is very tasty and can be used for soup of malfattini, rice with cabbage or beets, and maize; the broth can be improved by adding two sliced sausages to it.

The part of the turkey to be preferred for boiling is the front including the wings, which is the most delicate piece. For roast the rear parts are best adapted. For pot roast stick the meat with garlic and rosemary and season it with a fricassee of dry meat or lard, butter, salt and pepper, tomato sauce or tomato paste dissolved in water; use this fricassee to fry potatoes as a side-dish. Spit roast is to be smeared with oil and can be served with a side-dish of fried polenta. The breast of the turkey, flattened to a thickness of half an inch and seasoned with oil, salt and pepper, is excellent when grilled.

A young turkey of about 4 pounds can be roasted whole as a guinea-hen.

321 — STEAK, IN FLORENTINE STYLE

Put the steak on the gridiron over a bright coal fire; turn it many times; season with salt and pepper when it is done, and serve it with a small piece of butter on top. The steak must not be too well cooked, so that abundant juice flows from it when cut.

322 — FRIED STEAK

If the steak is not too tender, instead of grilling it, put it in a pot with a small piece of butter and a drop of oil, a clove of garlic and some rosemary. If necessary, add broth or water or tomato sauce. Serve the steak with diced potatoes cooked in the meat gravy.

PASTRY
323 — STRUDEL

Apples, 1 lb. 2 ounces
Flour, 9 ounces
Butter, 3½ ounces
Seedless raisins, 3 ounces
Powdered sugar, 3 ounces
Lemon rind
Cinnamon
Milk
1 Egg

Mix the flour with warm milk, butter the size of a nut, an egg, salt; make a firm dough and let it rest for half an hour in a luke-warm place.

Prepare the apples, remove the cores, and cut them into thin slices. Roll the dough into foil, cover the dough with the apples, add the raisins, lemon rind, cinnamon, sugar, and finally the butter, melted. Fold the dough up on both sides to form a stuffed roll; place this in a baking-pan, smeared with butter, and let the strudel follow the outlines of the pan. Smear the upper part of the dough with butter and put it in the oven.

324 — GATEAU A' LA NOISETTE

The pompous French name given to this dessert is very well suited, as it is indeed an excellent example of French pastry. The following are the ingredients for six or seven servings:

Flour of rice, 4 ounces
Sugar, 6 ounces
Butter, 3½ ounces
Sweet almonds, 1½ ounces
Shelled walnuts, 1½ ounces
Eggs, 4
Flavor of vanilla

Remove the skin from both the walnuts and the sweet almonds; dry them well either in the sun or near the fire and grind them finely. Add 2 tablespoonfuls of sugar and mix with the flour of rice. Beat the eggs with the remainder of the sugar. Mix everything and work the mixture energetically. Add the melted butter and continue to work the dough as before. Then place it in a medium-sized smooth round cake dish about three inches deep and bake it in the oven at moderate heat.

325 — BABA'

This dessert requires a great deal of attention, care and patience, but it will repay by the delicacy of its taste. Here is the list of ingredients:

Flour of Hungary or fine flour, 9 ounces (or less)
Powdered Sugar, 1 ounce
Grapes of Corinth (raisins) 1 ounce
A few Malaga grapes without seeds
Eggs, 2
Egg yolk, 1
Milk, ½ glass
Beer Yeast, size of a small egg
Marsala Wine, 1 tbsp.
A few thin slices of candied fruit
A pinch of salt
Flavor of vanilla
Butter, 3 ounces
Cognac, 1 tbsp.

Place the beer yeast in a handful of flour of Hungary, add a few drops of warm milk and work this into a rather solid roll. Place it near the moderate heat of the stove in a covered dish with a little milk and cut a cross on the dough so as to detect when it has raised. This should take about half an hour.

Break the eggs into a pan, add the sugar and beat well; add the rest of the flour, the beer yeast, the butter, melted and warm, the Marsala wine and cognac, and mix well. If the dough is hard, soften it with warm milk. Work it well with a wooden spoon until the dough separates from the pan by itself; add the raisins, the grapes and the sliced candied fruit. Place it in a cake dish twice as large as the loaf smeared with butter and flour. If possible, use a rib-shaped baking dish. Cover it air-tight and place it in a lukewarm stove, or country oven, to be raised. This will take about 2 hours. If the raising is successful, the loaf should be twice as big, that is, it should reach to the edge of the dish. Bake the cake without exposing it to the air. Stick a toothpick into it, and if the toothpick is dry when drawn out, the cake is done. but due to its thickness it must be left in the stove a while longer to allow it to dry in the tepid heat. If babà is baked properly, it should have the color of bread crust on the outside. Remove it from the dish, and spray it with confectionery sugar.

326 — FOILED MARCHPANE OR SWEET BREAD

Prepare dough for foils as described in No. 94. When the dough has been rolled into foil, cut two round pieces as large as an ordinary plate from it but leave a large fringed border of dough around the plate. On one of these spread the compound of sweet bread No. 334. Make the layer ¼ inch thick, and leave a margin around it. Place the other piece of foiled dough over it and close the edge with your finger, wet with water. Gild the surface of the foil crust with egg-yolks and bake it in the oven. When done, dash confectionery sugar on it.

This is sufficient for 7 or 8 servings.

327 — CRISPY COOKIES

Flour, 17 ounces
Confectionery sugar, 8 ounces (or less)
Sweet almonds, whole and peeled, mixed with some pine seeds (pinoli),
    4 ounces
Butter, ½ ounce
A pinch of anise
Eggs, 5
A pinch of salt

Put aside the almonds and pine-seeds (pinoli) and mix all the other ingredients with four eggs. Keep the other egg to soften the compound in case it is hard. Make four rolls out of the mixture, about ½ inch thick and four inches wide. Place them in a baking dish smeared with butter, spray them with flour and gild the top with egg-yolk. Place in the oven, but do not bake too well.

The following day cut them into slices, as the crust will have softened. Put the slices in the oven for a short time and remove them from the dish. The cookies will be crispy and delicious.

328 — SOFT COOKIES

To assure the proper size to these cookies and an even corner on both ends, use a dish of tin about four inches wide and the length of the oven.

Flour of Wheat, 1½ ounces
Flour of Potato, 1 ounce
Sugar, 3 ounces
Sweet Almonds 1½ ounces
Candied orange (or citron), ½ ounce
Thick fruit preserve of quince (or other jelly or fruit) ⅛ ounce
Eggs, 3

Peel the sweet almonds and cut them in two lengthwise. Dry them either in the sun or near the fire. (Some professional pastry cooks do not peel the almonds, but this is not a good practice, as the skin often sticks to the palate and is not easily digested.) Cut the candied orange and the fruit preserve into small squares. Mix the egg yolks, a little flour of wheat and the sugar together, and beat well for about half an hour. Beat the white of the eggs separately and add; then pour the flour through a sieve. Mix slowly and spread the almonds, the candied fruit and the fruit preserve into the compound. Smear a cake dish with butter, and dash a little flour on the surface before placing the compound in it. When baked, do not remove from dish. Slice the cookies the following day, and if preferred, toast them lightly in the oven.

329 — COOKIES, SULTAN STYLE

Confectionery Sugar, 5 ounces
Flour of Wheat, 3 ounces
Flour or Potato, 1½ ounces or less
Sultanine grapes (raisins), 3 ounces
Candied fruit, ⅛ ounce
Eggs, 5
Flavor of Lemon Rind
Cognac or rum, 2 tbsp.

Cut the candied fruit into pieces the size of watermelon seeds. Place them on the fire with the grapes barely covered with cognac. As soon as it boils, remove it from the fire, light the liquor, letting it burn until the cognac is entirely consumed. Remove the ingredients and dry them in a napkin. With a large spoon beat the egg yolks, the sugar and lemon rinds for half an hour. Beat the egg white till it thickens and add it to the compound. Add flour of wheat and flour of potato by passing them through a sieve, mixing slowly. Add the grapes, the candied fruit and 2 spoonfuls of cognac; pour the compound into a smooth, heavy, round metal dish smeared with butter and cover it with a veil-like layer of confectionery sugar of flour. Place it in the oven immediately to prevent the grapes and candied fruit from sinking to the bottom.

330 — BRIOCHES *(A sort of muffin)*

Flour of Hungary, 9 ounces
Butter, 5 ounces
Beer Yeast, ½ ounce
A pinch of Sugar
A very small pinch of Salt
Eggs, 3

Melt the beer yeast in tepid water and in ¼ of
the flour of Hungary. Form a solid, round loaf, cut
a cross on it and after spraying some flour on it, let
it raise in a moderately warm place in a small pan.

Place the remainder of the flour on a pastry
board. Make a hole in the middle and place the sugar,
salt and egg into it. Mix these ingredients with your
fingers and add butter, cut into small pieces. Begin
to mix the flour with the blade of a large knife, then
use your hand, adding the other two eggs, one at a
time. As soon as the raised yeast loaf has doubled in
size, add it to this dough, and knead it well into a
loaf. Spray a thin layer of flour under the loaf and
let it raise in a warm place free from draft. When the
loaf has become twice as big, place it on the pastry
board after spraying it with flour, and work it a while
with your hand covered with flour. Smear 16 or 18
striped tin muffin dishes, spray them with flour mixed with confectionery sugar, and fill each half with
dough. Place them in a lukewarm oven, and as soon
as the dough is raised to the brim of the dish. gild the
top with egg yolk and bake.

331— MARGUERITE BREAD

Flour of Potato, 4 ounces
Confectionery Sugar, 4 ounces
Eggs, 4
Flavor of lemon

Beat the egg yolks and the sugar thoroughly, add
the flour and lemon juice, and work it for half an
hour. Beat the egg whites, add them and mix very
slowly. Pour the compound into a smooth, round,

heavy metal dish, smeared with butter and sprayed with confectionery sugar, and place it in the oven at once. When baked, allow it to cool off before removing the baking dish from the oven. Spray with confectionery sugar and vanilla.

332 — PIE, MANTOVAN STYLE

Flour, 6 ounces
Sugar, 6 ounces
Butter, 5 ounces
One whole egg
Egg yolks, 4
Flavor of lemon rind
Sweet almonds and pine seeds, 2 ounces

Cut the pine-seeds in two crosswise. Peel the almonds in warm water and split them lengthwise; then cut the halves into four or five pieces.

Beat the eggs and sugar well with a long spoon; then pour the flour in gradually while working the compound. Add butter, melted in the steam. Place the compound into a copper dish smeared with butter and sprayed either with flour or bread crumbs, and spray the top with the pieces of almonds and pine-seeds. Bake in a moderate oven. See that the pie is not thicker than 1¼ inch so that it dries well. When baked, dash a veil of confectionery sugar over it and serve it cold.

333 — "CURLY" PIE I.

There are two recipes for curly pies, and each appeals to different tastes.

Peeled sweet almonds, mixed with a few bitter one, 4 ounces
Confectionery Sugar, 6 ounces
Candied fruit, 2½ ounces
Butter, 2 ounces
Lemon rinds
Flour
Eggs, 2

Mix two eggs with sufficient flour and make this into dough, cutting it into fine noodles, the kind prepared for chicken soup. In one corner of the pastry board make a heap of almonds, sugar, candied fruit (diced), and lemon grated finely. Chop all these ingredients together with a "lunette" chopper till they are reduced to the size of wheat grains, and flatten them with the rolling pin. Put a layer of noodles in the center of a large copper baking dish, spraying them with the chopped ingredients, and repeat the operation till you have a pie at least 1¼ inch thick. Add the melted butter with a brush to distribute it evenly on the surface and so that it may drip through thoroughly. Bake the pie, and when removed, dash a good deal of confectionery sugar on it while still warm. Serve it cold.

334 — "CURLY" PIE II.

Flour for crust, 6 ounces
Sugar, 2 ounces
Butter, less than 2 ounces
Lard, 1 ounce
Egg, 1

Use a copper baking dish, 12 inches in diameter. Smear it with butter. Place a piece of the dough as thick as a silver dollar in the form. Place marchepane or sweet bread made as follow on it:

Peeled sweet almonds, including 3 bitter almonds, 4 ounces
Sugar, 3½ ounces
Butter, ½ ounce
Candied orange, ½ ounce
Egg yolk, 1

Chop the almonds and sugar in the mortar, add the candied orange (diced), butter, egg yolk, and a tablespoon of water. Make a well-blended mixture. With the remainder of the crust dough make a wall in the dish by attaching it around the wall and edge with your finger wet with water. Spread the sweet bread equally at the bottom. Add a layer of fine noodles ¼ of an inch thick (but no more, as they are not the base of the pastry), and with a brush spread the top with ⅓ ounce of melted butter. Bake the pie in a moderate oven. When done, spread some diced candied citron on it, spray with confectionery sugar mixed with vanilla. Serve two days later, as time makes it softer and more delicate to the taste.

335 — MERINGUE PIE

Prepare some soft crust with half the quantities of recipe A of No. 341, and make a cream as follows:

Milk, 1 pint
Sugar, 2 ounces
Flour, 1 ounce
Eggs, 3
Flavor of Vanilla

Cut about 3½ ounces of very fine grade sponge cake into ¼ inch slices. Cover the bottom of a medium sized copper cake dish, smeared with butter, with soft crusting and with a finger (wet with water) make a wall of the same crusting around the dish, about ¼ inch thick and 1 inch high. Make a layer with half of the slices of sponge cake dipped into orange cordial. Spread the cream evenly and cover it with the remainder of the sponge cake slices, also basted with orange cordial (rosolio d'arancio). Beat the three egg whites left over from the cream, and when thick, add slowly 4 ounces of confectionery sugar. Stir the egg whites and sugar slowly, and cover the surface of the pie with it evenly, leaving the edge of the crusting untouched. Gild the edge crusting with egg yolk. Bake in oven, and when the meringue has become solid, cover it with a sheet of paper to prevent it from becoming too dark. Let the pie cool off before removing it from the dish, and sprinkle it lightly with confectionery sugar.

336 — PINE-SEED PIE *(Pinoli Pie)*

This is a pie that pastry shops sell in large quantities. Some may think it originated in the brain of a professor of the Sorbonne, but it is indeed a simple matter.

Milk, a little over 1 pint
Whole wheat flour, 3½ ounces
Sugar, 2 ounces
Pine-seeds (pinoli), 1½ ounces
Eggs, 2
A pinch of salt
Flavor of nutmeg
Butter

Chop the pine seeds as small as rice grains. Boil the whole wheat flour in milk, and when done, add the rest of the ingredients, leaving the eggs for the last, mixing very quickly and energetically. If the compound is not solid, add as much whole wheat flour as needed.

Make a soft crust with the following:

Flour, 7 ounces
Butter, 3½ ounces
Sugar, 3½ oz.
Egg, 1

Add, if necessary, a few drops of white wine or marsala wine to make the crusting softer. Smear a cake dish, 1¼ inch deep, with butter and cover the bottom with a thin layer of soft crusting. Pour in the compound and cover it with layers of cross-wise strips. Gild it and bake it in the oven. Serve it cold, sprayed with confectionery sugar.

337 — BOCCA DI DAMA I.
(Sweet Heart Cheek)

Some pastry cooks prepare this dessert without flour, but I suggest that it be used in order to assure consistency.

Powder sugar, 9 ounces
Flour (very fine), 5 ounces
Sweet Almonds, with a few bitter ones, 1½ ounces
Eggs, 6
Egg yolks, 3
Flavor of lemon rind

Peel the almonds and dry them well; then chop them finely together with a spoonful of sugar. Mix this with flour and see that there are no lumps. Place the remainder of the sugar in a pan, mix it with egg yolks and grated lemon rinds, and work it with a long spoon for 15 minutes. Add the flour and continue to work it for an hour.

Beat the six egg whites in a separate pan. When thick add them to the compound and mix slowly till everything is well blended. Pour the compound into a copper baking dish, smeared with butter; spray with confectionery sugar and flour and bake in oven at low fire.

338 — BOCCA DI DAMA II.
(Sweet Heart Cheek)

Sugar, 9 ounces
Very fine flour, 3½ ounces
Sweet almonds, with three bitter ones thrown in, 1½ ounces
Eggs, 9
Flavor of lemon rind

Peel the almonds, dry them well in the sun or near the fire; chop them finely together with a tablespoonful of sugar, and mix them with flour. Place the rest of the sugar in a copper pan, add the egg yolks and beat them with a regular egg beater on top of the stove (over a very low fire) for 15 minutes. Remove them from the stove and quickly add the flour, already mixed with almonds and the lemon rinds and continue to work. Beat the egg whites well and add. Mix slowly. Place the compound in a baking dish, smeared with butter and spread with flour. Bake in oven.

339 — NEAPOLITAN PASTRY

Aside from its delicate taste, this pastry makes a good show at the table. It is worthwhile following the instruction carefully.

Sugar, 4 oz.
Flour of Hungary, 4 oz.
Sweet almonds, 3 oz.
Eggs, 4

Remove the skin from the almonds and dry them in the sun or near the fire. Pick the largest of these, up to $\frac{1}{3}$ of the lot, and cut them into two lobes or halves; cut the rest into thin slices. Beat the eggs and sugar in a pan over a very low fire for 15 minutes Remove them from the fire and add the flour, mixing slowly. Use a smooth round baking dish, about 4 inches deep. Smear the baking dish with butter and spray it with a spoonful of powdered sugar and flour mixed together; pour in the compound. Bake in oven at moderate heat. Remove and cool. Cut into slices $\frac{1}{4}$ inch thick.

Now make a cream with the following ingredients:

Sugar, 2 oz.
Flour, $\frac{1}{2}$ oz.
Butter, $\frac{1}{2}$ oz.
Flavor of vanilla
Eggs, 2
Milk, less than 1 pint

Allow the butter and flour to cook over a low fire, but remove it before it browns. Wait till it becomes tepid, then add the egg yolks, milk and sugar. Replace on the fire, and when hot, spread it on one side of each slice of the cake and arrange the slices in layers (one on top of the other).

Now prepare a sort of frosting. Put 8 ounces of sugar and more than 1/5 pint of water in a pan. Stir to melt the sugar and heat till the liquid thickens so as to stick to your finger. Remove it as soon as it forms bubbles. As soon as it begins to cool, squeeze the juice of 1/4 of a lemon into it and work it with a large spoon until it becomes as white as snow. In case it is too thick, add sufficient water to thin it out so that it flows like thick heavy cream. Throw the almonds cut into thin slices into this frosting. Mix well and "plaster" the cake all around. On top of the cake make rows with the other almonds pieces, stuck straight up.

340 — GENOESE PASTRY

Sugar, 7 oz.
Butter, less than 5 oz.
Flour of Potato, 6 oz.
Flour of Wheat, 3½ oz.
Egg yolks, 12
Egg whites, 7
Flavor of lemon rind

Beat the egg yolks, butter and sugar in a pan; add the flour of potato and flour of wheat and work the entire compound for half an hour. Add the egg whites, well beaten. Smear a copper baking dish with

butter and spray it with flour. Make a layer about
½ inch thick and bake it in the oven. Cut the cake into
almond-shaped pieces and cover them with a veil of
powdered sugar.

341 — CRUSTINGS

Here are three recipes for three different crustings.
It is suggested that the third one be prepared, as it is
the finest, especially for crusting of delicious pastry.

Recipe A

Flour, 17 oz.
White sugar, a little over 7 oz.
Butter, less than 6 oz.
Lard, less than 2 oz.
Eggs, 2
Egg yolk, 1

Recipe B

Flour, 9 oz.
Butter, 4½ oz.
White sugar, 3½ oz.
Egg, 1
Egg yolk, 1

Recipe·C

Flour, 9½ oz.
Sugar, 4 oz.
Butter, 3 oz.
Lard, 1½ oz.
Egg yolks, 4

The following is the simplest way to make soft crusting. Grind the sugar finely, mix it with the flour, and soften the butter by working it with a wet hand. Now make a loaf of all the ingredients by using the blade of a large knife in mixing them. Do not work it too much or too long. Whenever possible, it is advisable to prepare this crusting the day before, as time is in its favor, and when baked, it is softer and mealy.

When about to use the crusting for the pastry, flatten it to the desired thickness with a rolling pin. If you wish to give it the appearance of fancy pastry, use the "grooved" rolling pin on the side of the crusting which goes outside in your last touches. The use of powdered sugar in stretching the dough will make it easier to handle. Adding a few drops of white wine or marsala wine to the leavings and mixing them with the main loaf will make the crusting softer.

342 — CORNFLOUR CAKES

Cornflour, 7 oz.
Flour of wheat, over 5 oz.
Powdered sugar, 5 oz.
Butter, 3 oz.
Lard, less than 2 oz.
Anise, ⅛ oz.
Egg, 1

Mix the corn and the wheat flour together. With the anise, sugar, lard and egg mix as much of the mixed flours as possible in order to form a loaf. Place this loaf aside for the time being. Add a few drops of white wine to the leavings, work it for a while, and form it into a separate loaf. Now mix the two loaves together, work the dough a little to retain its softness. Flatten it with the rolling pin to thickness of ¼ of an inch, spray it with flour to prevent it from sticking to the board, and cut it into a variety of shapes and sizes. Smear a pie dish with lard, spray it with flour and put the cakes in, gilt them with egg yolks. Bake in the oven and spray with powdered sugar.

343 — CENCI *(Rags)*

Flour, 9 oz.
Butter, ⅔ oz.
Powdered sugar, ⅔ oz.
Eggs, 2
Brandy, 1 spoonful
A pinch of salt

Mix these ingredients into a rather solid loaf, work it thoroughly with your hand. Spray it with flour, wrap it in a canvas or napkin, and allow it to rest. If it is too soft, add some flour. Roll it with the rolling pin to the thickness of a silver dollar, and cut it with the pastry wheel into pieces four inches long and two inches wide. Make a few cuts on each, and arrange them in as many fancy shapes as you can. Cook in either lard or oil, but be sure that they boil in it (like French-fried potatoes). Dash powdered sugar on them while still hot. This quantity is sufficient for a large dish.

344 — LIVORNESE CAKE
(Stiacciata alla Livornese)

These cakes are popular at Easter time. In that mild Spring season the raising of the dough is easier, and the housewife will not risk her work and ingredients, as this cake requires prolonged and careful manipulation, favored by mild temperature. The following quantity of ingredients is sufficient for three medium-sized cakes:

Eggs, 12
Very fine flour, 4 lbs.
Sugar, 1⅓ lbs.
Pure olive oil, ½ pint
Butter, 2 oz.
Beer yeast, ¾ oz.
Anise, ⅓ oz.
Vino santo (old raisins wine), ⅓ pt.
Marsala wine, ¼ pt.
Orange flour water, ⅔ pt.

Follow carefully the operations described:

1. — Mix the two wines and wash the anise thoroughly. Take a small portion of the wine in a separate dish and place the anise in it, allowing it to soak. Melt the beer yeast in a half glass of lukewarm water, and add as much flour as necessary to form a consistent loaf. Heap the rest of the flour in a pan, put the yeast loaf on it and cover it with flour. Keep the pan at moderate kitchen temperature during the night.

2. — In the morning, when the yeast loaf is well raised, place it on the pastry board, spread it,

and add one egg, a spoonful of oil, a spoonful of sugar, a spoonful of wine, and enough flour to form a larger loaf. Mix everything well, but do not work it too much. Replace it on the flour and cover it as before. Allow it to raise for six or seven hours.

3. — After seven hours add 3 egg, three spoonfuls of oil, three of sugar, three of vine and some flour. Cover as before. Allow it to raise.

4. — Remove the loaf. Add five eggs, five spoonfuls of sugar, five of oil, five of wine, and the necessary flour. Allow it to raise again.

5. — Mix the remaining three eggs, the butter and the rest of the ingredients, melting the butter on a low fire. Add this to the loaf. Work well and form a well-blended loaf. If too soft, add enough flour to make it consistent.

Divide the loaf into three or four parts. Form them into four round loaves. Place each in a separate baking dish, smeared with butter and covered with a sheet of paper up to the edge. Be sure that the dish is large enough to allow raising expansion. Now, due to the periodical addition of ingredients, the raising takes longer. If you wish to hasten it, place the dishes in warm water. When raised, the dough appears to quiver when the dish is handled. Now, using a brush, smear the surface first with orange flower water, and then, using the same brush, with egg yolk.

Bake in a very moderate oven. Since it is a thick loaf, the temperature must always be evenly low in order to assure the proper baking of the inside of the cake.

If the above operations are carried out carefully,

these home-made Livornese cakes will be even more delicious than the famous ones of Burchi of Pisa.

345 — SPONGE CAKE

Eggs, 6
Powderer sugar, 6 oz.
Flour of Hungary, 6 oz.
Lemon rind flavoring

Mix the egg yolks with the sugar, and add the flour which has been dried in the sun or near the fire. Work the dough for about half an hour, add two spoonfuls of the beaten egg whites to soften the compound, and finally the remaining whites, mixing slowly.

346 — BISCUIT (Biscotto)

Eggs, 6
Powdered sugar, ½ lb.
Wholewheat flour, 3½ oz.
Potato flour, almost 2 oz.
Lemon rind flavoring

Stir the egg yolks, the sugar and a spoonful of two kinds of flour for at least half an hour. Beat the egg whites and add: mix slowly, and when the compound is uniform, pour in the flour through a sieve. The flour must have been dried in the sun or near the fire.

Smear a baking-pan with butter and spray it with powdered sugar and flour. Bake the biscuit until it is raised about 2 in.

347 — CHOCOLATE BISCUIT

Eggs, 6
Powdered sugar, 7 oz.
Wholewheat flour, 5 oz.
Chocolate, almost 2 oz.

Grate the chocolate and mix it with the sugar and the egg yolks. Add the flour and work the.compound for more than half an hour. Finally add the beaten egg whites, mixing slowly.

348 — PASTA MADDALENA

Sugar 4½ oz.
Fine flour, 3 oz.
Butter, 1 oz.
Egg yolks, 4
Egg whites, 3
A pinch of bicarbonate of soda
Lemon rind flavoring

Mix the egg yolks with the sugar, and when they have become whitish add the flour and stir for another fifteen minutes. Add the melted butter and finally the beaten egg whites.

Various shapes can be given to the dough but it must not exceed a thickness of about ¼ inch. Cut the dough into cookies with a ready-made form, or bake it first and then cut it into diamond-shaped pieces and spray them with sugar.

349 — PIZZA, IN NEAPOLITAN STYLE

Sugar, 2 oz.
Flour, less than 1 oz.
Eggs, 1 and 1 yolk
Lemon rind flavoring
Milk, half a glass
Ricotta, 5 oz.
Almonds, sweet and three bitter, 2 oz.

Make a custard with the milk, the sugar, the flour and the egg. When it is cooked and still boiling, add the yolk and the flavoring. Then add the ricotta and the almonds, ground finely. Use crusting No. 341, B.

Mix everything and fill the crusting arranged in the shape of a pie. Gild the upper crust of the pie with an egg yolk, and bake in the oven. Serve cold, sprayed with confectionery sugar.

350 — STUFFED PIZZA

The custard filling is made of the following ingredients:

Milk, ½ pint
Sugar, 2 oz.
Starch, 1 oz.
Two egg yolks
Any flavoring

Add the following to the custard when removing it from the fire:

Whole Pinoli, 1 oz.
Raisins, 2½ oz.

Fill a pie with this compound, as in the preceding recipe.

351 — PIES (Crostate)

The crusts of these pies are made of foliated dough and the filling consists of fruit preserves or custard.
For the crusting use Recipe C. No. 341. Roll out half of the dough with a plain rolling pin, to form a round crust of the thickness of a silver dollar; put it in a baking-pan smeared with butter. Spread a

layer of preserve or of cream on the crust. If the preserve is too thick, soften it on the fire with water. On top of the preserve place strips of dough about ¼ inch wide crosswise; cover the ends of the strips with a ring of dough, wetting it with water to attach it well. Gild the upper parts of the crusting with egg yolk, and bake the pie in the oven.

352 — ALMOND CAKE
(Croccante)

Sweet almonds, 4 ounces
Powdered sugar, 3½ ounces

Peel the almonds, separate the lobes and cut them into thin strips. Put the almonds on the fire and dry them until they become yellow, without however roasting. Put the sugar on the fire and when it is melted pour in the almonds, warm and well mixed. The croccante is done when it takes on the color of cinnamon. Pour it, a little at a time, into a cake form smeared with butter and oil, and press it against the walls of the dish with a lemon, so that it becomes as thin as possible. Remove it from the cake form when it is cold, and if this should be difficult place the dish in boiling water.

353 — SPONGE CAKE ROLL
(Salame inglese)

Prepare a sponge cake with the following ingredients. To bake it place it in a rectangular baking-dish smeared with butter and sprayed with flour; the dough should not be more than ⅛ inch thick.

Powdered sugar, 7 ounces
Fine flour, 6 ounces
Eggs, 6

Dry the flour well before using it to make it lighter.

Beat the egg yolks with the sugar for about half an hour; add the beaten egg whites and then pour in the flour through a sieve. When the cake is still hot cut strips from it, 1 inch wide and as long as the roll to which they are to serve as stuffing. These strips should be of different colors; wet some with white rosolio so that they remain yellow; others with alkermes to become red; the rest can be made black with white rosolio mixed with chocolate. Cover the strips with a liquid fruit preserve; place them one on top of the other alternating colors, in the middle of the sponge cake of which the surface is also spread with preserve.

Pull the ends of the sponge cake over the strips and form a roll, which when sliced shows a checkerboard of various colors.

For family use this recipe can be simplified. Use only half of the ingredients.

Cover the sponge cake with rosolio and fruit preserve; place thin slices of candied fruit on the preserve, and roll the cake up.

In both cases it is well to ornament the upper part with a sugar frosting or a chocolate coating.

Mix some powdered sugar with an egg white so

that it is very thick and spread it on the roll uniformly. For a chocolate frosting take 2 ounces of sugar and 1 ounce of chocolate; mix well, add an egg white and spread it on the cake. If it does not dry naturally, place it near moderate heat.

354 — ALMOND COOKIES I.
(Amaretti)

Powdered sugar. 8½ ounces
Sweet almonds, 3½ ounces
Bitter almonds, less than 2 ounces
Egg whites, 2

Peel the almonds and dry them in the sun or near the fire; chop them well. Stir the sugar and the egg whites for at least half an hour; add the almonds to form a thick dough; make balls the size of a nut from the dough. If the dough is too soft, add sugar; if it is too hard some beaten egg white. To give a darker color to the amaretti, add burnt sugar.

Place the dough balls in a baking-pan smeared with butter and sprayed with flour and powdered sugar. Place them far apart, as they spread and puff up.

Bake in a moderate oven.

355 — ALMOND COOKIES II.

Powdered sugar, 10½ ounces
Sweet almonds, 6 ounces
Bitter almonds, less than 1 ounce
Egg whites, 2

Peel the almonds and dry them in the sun or near the fire. Pound them in a mortar with an egg white, pouring in a little at a time. Add half of the sugar, working the compound with the hand. Pour it in a bowl, add half of an egg white, then the rest of the sugar, and finally the other half of the egg white, stirring constantly.

Form the dough into an even roll and cut it into equal pieces. Make dough balls, the size of a nut, out of these pieces, touching them with wet hands. Flatten the balls and follow the directions of the preceding recipe. Spray the cookies with powdered sugar before putting them into a very hot stove.

This recipe will make about thirty amaretti.

356 — RICE CAKES
(Pasticcini di riso)

Rice, 5 ounces
Sugar, 2½ ounces
Butter, 1 ounce
Candied fruit, 1 ounce
Milk, 4|5 quart
Eggs, 3
Rum, 2 spoonfuls
Salt

Cook the rice, stirring it often so that it does not stick to the pot. When it is two-thirds done add the sugar, the butter, the salt, and the candied fruit cut into pieces. When it is done and has cooled off, add the rum, the egg yolks, and the beaten egg whites.

Take grooved individual baking cups, smear

them with butter, spray with bread crumbs, fill them and bake in a country oven.

This recipe will make 12 or 14 cakes.

357 — SEMOLINO CAKES

Semolino, 6 ounces
Sugar, 3½ ounces
Pine seeds, 1½ ounces
Butter, less than 1 ounce
Milk, 4|5 quart
Eggs, 4
Salt
Lemon rind flavoring

Cook the semolino in the milk, and when it begins to thicken, throw in the pine seeds which have been pounded in a mortar together with the sugar; add the butter and the rest of the ingredients except the eggs. Add the eggs when the mixture is cold. For the rest follow the directions of the preceding recipe.

The ingredients are sufficient for 18 or 20 cakes.

358 — TEA CAKES

(Pastine pel thè)

Flour of Hungary, 1 pound
Potato flour, 5½ ounces
Powdered sugar, 5½ ounces
Butter, 5½ ounces
Egg whites, 2
Warm milk

Mix the two flours with sugar, and place this in a mound on the pastry-board. Make a hole in the middle, and put the egg whites and the butter (in pieces) into it. Work the dough for about half an hour; add enough milk to make it rather soft. Roll it out to the thickness of a silver dollar, cut it into discs; make holes in these discs with a fork and bake them in a baking-pan smeared with butter.

359 — RICE PIE

Milk, 1 quart
Rice, 7 ounces
Sugar 5 ounces
Sweet almonds, with 4 bitter ones, 3½ ounces
Candied citron, 1 ounce
Whole eggs, 3
Egg yolks, 5
Lemon rind flavoring
Salt

Peel the almonds and pound them in a mortar together with 2 tablespoonfuls of sugar.

Cut the candied citron into very small squares.

Cook the rice in the milk and when it is solid add the other ingredients. Add the eggs when the rice is cold.

Place the mixture in a baking pan smeared with butter and sprayed with bread crumbs; bake it in the oven. Cut it into almond-shaped pieces the day after, and spray it with powdered sugar before serving.

360 — RICOTTA PIE
(Torta di ricotta)

Ricotta (Sweet cottage cheese), 17½ ounces
Sugar, 5 ounces
Sweet almonds, 5 ounces
Bitter almonds, 4 or 5
Whole eggs, 4
Egg yolks, 4
Vanilla flavoring

Peel the almonds in warm water; pound them in a mortar with one of the egg whites; pass them through a fine sieve. Mix the almonds with the ricotta to form a smooth paste. Mix the sugar and eggs and add them to the compound.

Smear a baking-pan with lard and line it with a simple dough made of flour, water and sugar. Pour the compound on it, to the thickness of about ¾ inch. Bake between two fires or in the oven. The heat must be very moderate; keep a sheet of paper smeared with butter on the ricotta, so that it remains white. When it is cold, cut it into almond-shaped pieces; the dough crust can be eaten or not according to preference.

This recipe is sufficient for 12 or more persons.

361 — POTATO PIE
(Torta di Patate)

Potatoes, large and mealy, 1½ pounds
Sugar, 5 ounces
Sweet almonds, with 3 bitter ones, 2½ ounces
Eggs, 5
Salt
Lemon rind flavoring

Boil the potatoes, peel them, and pass them through a sieve while they are still warm. Peel the almonds and chop them finely together with the sugar. Add them to the potatoes with the other ingredients. Work everything well for a whole hour, adding the eggs one at a time. Smear a baking-pan with butter and spray it with bread crumbs; pour in the mixture and bake. Serve cold the following day.

362 — SEMOLINO PIE

Milk, 1 quart
Semolino, fine-grained, 4½ ounces
Sugar, 4½ ounces
Sweet almonds, with 3 bitter ones, 3½ ounces
Butter, less than 1 ounce
Eggs, 4
Lemon rind, ground
Salt

Peel the almonds in warm water; grind them very fine in a mortar, together with the sugar which is added one spoonful at a time.

Cook the semolino in the milk and add the butter and the almonds before removing it from the fire. Salt and add the beaten eggs when the semolino has cooled off. Pour the mixture in a baking-dish smeared with butter and sprayed with bread crumbs. The pie should not be thicker than 1¼ inches. Bake in the oven; remove the pie when cold and serve it cold or cut into pieces.

363 — CURRANTS, IN ENGLISH STYLE

Currants, 10½ ounces
Sugar, 4 ounces
Water, less than ½ pint

Remove the stems from the currants, put them on the fire with the water, and add the sugar when they are boiling. Do not let them boil for more than 2 minutes. Serve the ribes cold, as cooked fruit.

Maraschino cherries can be prepared in the same way, without removing the pits. Add a cinnamon stick to the water.

364 — SEMOLINO PUDDING

Milk, 4|5 quart
Semolino, 5 ounces
Sugar, 3½ ounces
Raisins, 3½ ounces
Butter, less than 1 ounce
Eggs. 4
Rum, 3 tablespoonfuls
Salt
Lemon rind flavoring

Cook in a simple or grooved pan; smeared with butter and sprayed with grated bread. Serve hot.

365 — RICE PUDDING

Milk, 1 quart
Rice, 5½ ounces
Sugar, 3½ ounces
Seedless raisins, 2½ ounces
Candied fruit, 1 ounce
Eggs, 2 whole ones and 2 yolks
Rum or cognac, a small glassful
Vanilla flavoring

Cook the rice in the milk; when it is half-done add the sugar, the raisins, the candied fruit cut into very small pieces, salt and butter. Remove it from the fire when it is done; while still warm add the eggs, the rum and the vanilla, mixing everything well. Bake, as for the other recipes.

As the rice hardens add milk.

366 — RICOTTA PUDDING

Ricotta (sweet cottage cheese), 10 ounces
Powdered sugar 3½ ounces
Sweet almonds, 3½ ounces
Bitter almonds, 3 or 4
Eggs, 5
Lemon rind flavoring

Peel the almonds in warm water and pound them in the mortar together with one of the egg whites. Pass the ricotta through a sieve and mix it with almonds. Beat the eggs with the sugar and add them to the mixture. Pour it into a baking-pan smeared with butter and sprayed with grated bread.

Serve cold.

This portion is sufficient for 6 or 7 persons.

367 — PUDDING, IN NEAPOLITAN STYLE

Cook some semolino in 3 glasses of water; it should not be too thick. Remove it from the fire, season it with sugar, salt and lemon rind flavoring, and when it has cooled off somewhat add 3 egg yolks and 2 egg whites. Mix well. Take a copper baking-pan of medium size, smear it with butter and line it with a crusting, the thickness of a silver dollar, (half of recipe A, No. 341 is sufficient). Pour in ⅓ of the semolino and scatter some preserved fruits on it-such as apricot, quince and raspberry preserves. Add two more layers of semolino, alternating with the preserves. Cover the pudding with crusting and wet the edges of the dough so that they stick together well. Ornament the surface of the pie, gild it with egg yolk and bake it in the oven. Spray it with powdered sugar on removing, and serve it cold.

368 — LEMON PUDDING

One large lemon
Sugar, 6 ounces
Sweet almonds, with 3 bitter ones, 6 ounces
Eggs, 6
Rum or cognac, 1 teaspoonful

Cook the lemon in water for about 2 hours: remove it dry and pass it through a sieve. If it is very bitter. keep it in cold water while still whole. Add the sugar, the almonds, peeled and ground very fine, the 6 egg yolks and the rum. Mix everything well; beat egg whites and add them to the compound. Cook as other puddings.

369 — CHOCOLATE PUDDING

Milk 4|5 quart
Sugar. almost 3 ounces
Chocolate, 2 ounces
Lady Fingers, 2 ounces
Eggs. 3
Vanilla flavoring

Grate the chocolate and put it into the milk. When it begins to boil add the sugar and the Lady Fingers broken into small pieces. Stir from time to time so that the mixture does not stick to the pot. Remove it from the fire after half an hour and pass it through a sieve. When it is cold, add the beaten eggs and the vanilla, pour it into a plain pan whose bottom has been covered by liquefied powdered sugar. Cook in bain marie style.

½ ounces of sugar is sufficient to cover the bottom of the pan.

370 — TOASTED ALMONDS PUDDING

Milk, 4|5 quart
Sugar, 3½ ounces
Sweet almonds, 2 ounces
Lady Fingers, 2 ounces
Eggs, 3

First prepare the almonds. Peel them in warm water and toast them; chop them very finely and add them to the compound as in the preceding recipe.

The toasted almonds will give an ashy color to the pudding and their taste will call forth praise.

This pudding can be frozen before being served and can be covered with cream.

371 — BIANCO MANGIARE

Sweet Almonds, including 3 bitter ones, 5 ounces
Powdered sugar, 5 ounces
Isinglass, ¾ ounce
Heavy cream, half a glass
Water, 1½ glasses
Orange blossom water, 2 spoonfuls

First prepare the isinglass; press it into the bottom of a glass, cover it with water and let it stand so that it softens up. To use it, throw away the water and wash the isinglass. Peel the almonds and grind them in a mortar, adding water from time to time. When they are ground very fine, dilute them in water and pass them through a cloth, pressing out all the substance. Put the almonds, the cream, the sugar, the isinglass and the orange on the fire; stir and allow to boil for a few minutes. Remove the mixture from the fire; when it has cooled off, pour it into a mould immersed in cold water or ice.

To remove from the mould place a cloth wet with boiling water around it.

372—CAKE TO BE SERVED WITH ZABAIONE

Potato flour, 1¾ ounces
Wheat flour, ¾ ounce
Powdered sugar, 3 ounces
Eggs, 3
Lemon rind flavor

Beat the egg yolks with the sugar for about half an hour, add the well beaten egg whites and pour in the flour through a sieve. Mix everything, but keep compound light. Smear a mould with a hole in the middle with butter and spray it with flour and powdered sugar. Pour in the compound and put it in the oven immediately.

Remove it from the mould when cold and pour zabaione into the hole in the center. Serve immediately.

373 — CREAM

Milk, 1 quart
Sugar, 7 ounces
Egg yolks, 8
Vanilla flavoring

Mix the egg yolks with the sugar and add the milk a little at a time. Cook the cream on a bright fire, but turn the fire down when the compound begins to smoke. The cream is done when it sticks to the laddle, which must be moved continually. Add the vanilla shortly before removing from the fire.

This recipe can be used for ice creams.

To improve the taste add bits of candied fruit, sliced very thinly.

374 — WHIPPED CUSTARD

Egg yolks, 6
Powdered sugar, 2½ ounces
Isinglass, ½ ounce
Water, ¾ of a glass
Cherry-laurel leaves, 3

Mix the egg yolks and the sugar in a casserole, add the water and the cherry-laurel leaves and put on the fire stirring continually until cooked. The cream is done when it condenses and when it remains attached to the ladle. Pour it into a dish and beat it up while still hot. Remove the cherry leaves and pour in the isinglass a little at a time, continuing to beat. If the cream does not whip well, place the dish on ice. Take a grooved mould, smear it with oil, surround it with ice, and pour in the whipped custard, placing lady fingers, dipped in rosolio or spread with fruit preserve, in the cream, if so preferred. Leave it in the ice for more than an hour, and remove it from the mould.

The isinglass it to be prepared as follows: place it in water first, then on the fire until the water evaporates partly, and a condensed liquid remains. This liquid is to be added to the cream while still boiling.

This recipe is sufficient for 5 or 6 persons.

375 — MIGLIACCIO DI ROMAGNA

Milk, 7|10 quart
Honey, 7 ounces
Sweet almonds, shelled, 3½ ounces
Sugar, 3½ ounces
Grated bread, very fine, 2¾ ounces
Candied fruit 1¾ ounces
Butter, 1¾ ounces
Fine spices, 2 teaspoons
Chocolate, 3½ ounces
Nutmeg, 1 teaspoon
Lemon rind
Blood of pork, 12 ounces

Cut the candied fruit into small pieces and grind it in a mortar, together with the almonds, adding a teaspoon of milk from time to time. Pass through a sieve. Put the milk on the fire with the lemon rind; remove the lemon and let the milk boil for 10 minutes. Add the grated chocolate, and when it has dissolved, remove the milk from the fire and let it cool off. Pass the blood through a sieve and add it to the milk together with all the other ingredients; add the grated bread last.

Cook the mixture in double boiler style, stirring often so that it does not stick. It is done, when the ladle stands straight up in the middle of the pot. Pour the mixture in a baking-pan, lined with simple dough and cut it into almond-shaped pieces when cold. Do not bake the dough too much and do not let the migliaccio get dry. Remove from the oven when a toothpick stuck into the pie remains clean.

376 — STUFFED PEACHES

Peaches, large and not too ripe, 6
Small lady fingers, 4
Powdered sugar, 2¾ ounces
Sweet almonds, with 3 peach almonds, 1¾ ounces
Orange or citron peel, 1|5 ounce
White wine, half a glass

Cut peaches in half, remove the stones, enlarge the holes where the pits were. Peel the almonds, add the removed pulp, and grind them very fine in a mortar together with 1¾ ounces of the sugar. Add the lady fingers broken into crumbs, and the candied fruit diced very small. Fill the center holes of the peaches with this mixture and place them in a pan, side by side, with filling at the top. Pour in the wine and the remaining sugar and cook between two fires.

Serve either warm or cold in their own syrup.

377 — APPLES IN JELLY

Take rennet apples or apples of fine quality, not too large and ripe. Remove the core, pare them, and throw them into cold water in which half a lemon has been squeezed. If there are about 1½ pounds of apples, dissolve 4 ounces of sugar in a pint of water to which a spoonful of kirsch has been added. Pour the sugar on the apples lined up evenly in a casserole. Cook so that the apples remain whole, remove them dry, place them on a fruit dish, and when they are cold fill the holes left by the removal of the cores with currant jelly. Reduce the liquid left in the casserole to a syrup, strain it through a wet cloth, add another spoonful of kirsch and pour the syrup around the apples. Serve cold.

Rosolio can be substituted for kirsch and fruit preserves for the currant jelly.

— 378 — APRICOTS IN SYRUP
(Albicocche in Composta)

Apricots, not ripe, 1 pound 5 ounces
Powdered sugar, 3½ ounces
Water, 1 glass

Remove the stones from the apricots carefully, and put them on the fire with the water.

When the water begins to boil, add the sugar; continue cooking, stirring from time to time.

When the apricots are soft and somewhat wrinkled, remove them one by one and place them in a fruit dish. Continue boiling the water which is still in the pot, and when it has condensed to a thick syrup pour it on the apricots.

379 — PEARS IN SYRUP
(Pere in Composta)

Pears, 1 pound 5 ounces
Powdered sugar, 4 ounces
Water, 2 glasses
Lemon, ½

If the pears are small, leave them whole with the stem; if they are large cut them in slices. Pare them and place them in the water into which the lemon has been squeezed: this should preserve the whiteness of the fruit. Strain the water and let the pears cook in it; add the sugar when the water begins to boil. For the rest follow the directions of the preceding recipe.

380 — SURPRISE CAKE
(Pasticcio a Sorpresa)

Milk, 1 quart
Rice flour, 7 ounces
Sugar, 4 ounces
Butter, ¾ ounce
Eggs, 6
Salt
Vanilla flavoring

Pour the eggs, the sugar, the flour and the milk little by little into a casserole. Stir continually so that no lumps are formed. Put the casserole on the fire and continue stirring; add the butter, the vanilla and the salt before removing the cream from the fire. Let it cool off and then pour it into a metal dish, to that it is rounded at the top.

Cover it with foil dough No. 341, B, ornament it in some way, gild it with egg yolk and bake it in the oven. Serve warm, sprayed with powdered sugar.

381 — ZABAIONE

Egg yolks, 3
Powdered sugar, 2 ounces
Marsala or Madera wine, 6 spoonfuls
Rum, 1 spoonful, if desired
Cinnamon, 1 teaspoon

Beat the egg yolks with the sugar, until they are almost white. Add the wine, mix, and put it on a bright fire. Stir continually; do not allow to boil; remove it when it begins to rise.

This recipe is sufficient for 4 persons, if served in glasses.

382 — ORZATA
(Barley Water)

Sweet almonds, with 10 or 12 bitter ones, 7 ounces
Water, 1 pound 5 ounces
Fine sugar, 1¾ pounds
Orange blossom water, 2 spoonfuls

Peel the almonds and grind them in a mortar, adding orange blossom water a little at a time. When they are reduced to a paste, dilute them in ⅓ of the orange water and pass them through a cloth. Put the dry paste back in the mortar, dilute it with another ⅓ of the water, and strain it. Repeat the operation a third time, put all the liquid obtained on the fire. When it is hot add the sugar, mix it, and let it boil for 20 minutes. When it is cold, pour it into a bottle and keep it in a cool place. It will keep for a long time without fermenting, but not as long as fruit syrups. A very small quantity, dissolved in a glass of water, will make an excellent refreshing drink.

383 — APRICOT PRESERVE

Take apricots that are very ripe and of good quality. Remove the stones, and put them on the fire without water. Stir them while they boil so as to ınash them. When they have boiled for about half an hour, strain them to remove the skin. Put them on the fire again with powdered sugar in the proportion of 8 to 10, about 13 ounces of sugar to 1 pound of strained apricots. Stir often until the consistency of preserves is reached; this is recognized if a spoonful of the mixture poured on a plate flows slowly.

Pour the warm preserve into jars, and when it is cold cover them with tissue paper immersed in alcohol; close the opening of the jar with thick paper tied around the neck.

Follow the same directions for peach preserve.

If the preserve moulds, it is an indication that the fruit was not sufficiently cooked. To remedy this situation put them on the fire again.

384 — ROSOLIO

Powdered sugar, 1⅛ pounds
Water, 12 ounces
Alcohol, at 36 degrees, 9 ounces
Saffron
Orange, 1

Remove the outside peel of the orange and place it in the alcohol, together with the saffron; leave it in a jug covered with a perforated sheet of paper for three days. Place the sugar and the water in another jug, stir it from time to time so that the sugar dissolves. On the fourth day mix the two liquids, and let them stand for another eight days. Strain the rosolio through a cloth and bottle it.

385 — MACEDONIA

Take various fruits in season, ripe and of good quality: currants, strawberries, raspberries, cherries, raisins, apricots, 1 peach, 1 pear. Start with the cherries and peel the fruits, cut them into small slices, and throw away the cores and stones. Use very little currants, because of their large seeds.

If the fruit prepared in this way weighs about 1 pound, spray 3½ ounces of sugar on it and the juice of 1 lemon. Mix and let rest for half an hour. Place a sheet of paper in the bottom of an ice-cream mould, fill it with the fruit, pressing somewhat; close the mould and put it in ice and salt for at least an hour and a half. When it is removed from the mould it should appear like a piece of marble of ice-cream.

This recipe is sufficient for 4 or 5 persons.

386 — QUINCE PRESERVE

Quinces, with the skin and core removed, 1¾ pounds
Powdered sugar, 1 pound

Dilute the sugar with half a glass of water, boil it for a while, and put it aside.

Cut the quinces into very thin slices and put them on the fire with a glass of water. Keep them covered but stir them often mashing them with the ladle. When they have become soft, pour in the sugar syrup, stir often and let them boil uncovered. The preserve is done when it is thick enough to remain standing when taken up with the ladle.

INDEX